CANTERBURY CHRIST CHURCH UNIVERSITY

THE FIRST FORTY-FIVE YEARS

Canterbury Christ Church University

The First Forty-Five Years

Nigel Watson

Canterbury Christ Church University: the first forty-five years

First published in 2007 by James and James (Publishers) Ltd,
a member of Third Millennium Information Group

2–5 Benjamin Street
London
United Kingdom
EC1M 5QL
www.tmiltd.com

ISBN: 978 1 903942 82 6

British Library Cataloguing in Publication Data
A CIP catalogue record for this book is available from the British Library.

Project editor: Susan Millership
Image research: Susan and Iona Millership
Designer: Susan Pugsley
Production manager: Bonnie Murray

Reprographics: Asia Graphic Printing Ltd
Printer: Butler and Tanner, Frome, Somerset

Previous page: The chapel doors.
Right: Students on campus.

Contents

Foreword by the Vice Chancellor 6

Introduction 8

Beginnings 1962–1976 12

Diversification 1977–1989 46

Expansion 1989–1997 72

University 1997–Onwards 98

Appendices 140

Index 142

Foreword

Since its founding in 1962 as a teacher training college, Canterbury Christ Church has enjoyed a remarkable and extraordinarily successful period of growth and development. This book sets out the events, activities and achievements which have taken place during this time. However, the book is not simply meant to be a record of what happened. It is equally a testimony to the many people, staff and students alike, whose skill and efforts have enabled Christ Church to be what its mission envisages:

> *Inspired by the University's Church of England Foundation and the aspirations of its students and staff, our mission is to pursue excellence in academic and professional higher education thereby enriching both individuals and society.*

The book also offers a perspective on the way in which British higher education developed in the latter half of the twentieth century.

Considerable work lies behind the publication of the book and the efforts and contribution of all those involved are acknowledged. Particular thanks go to Hamish McGibbon (James and James), Nigel Watson (author), Susan Millership (project editor) and to Linda Hinde who has coordinated the project on behalf of the University. We are also indebted to Professor Chris Bounds (formerly the Deputy Vice Chancellor) whose long association with Christ Church enabled him to provide us with invaluable advice.

I do hope you find the book informative and enjoyable.

Professor Michael Wright
Vice Chancellor
October 2007

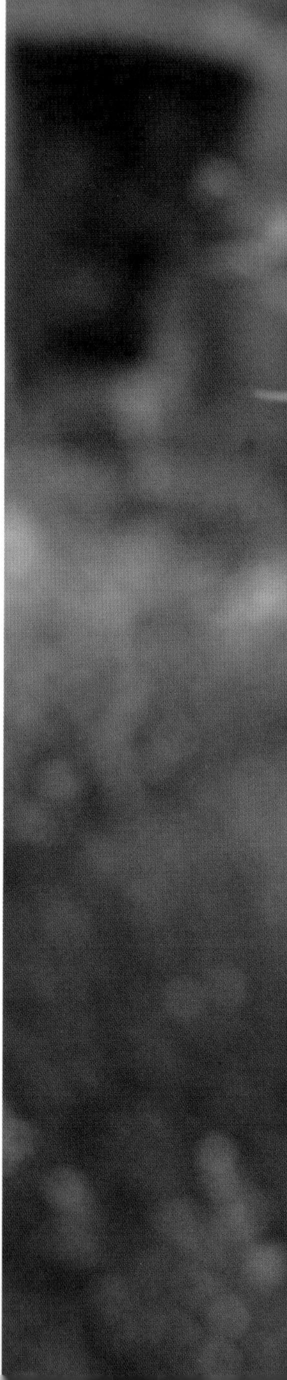

Introduction

Canterbury Christ Church University joined the ranks of Britain's universities in the summer of 2005. It was already a successful institution, with over 14,000 students, a prime reputation in delivering professional training in education, health and social care and policing, and a demonstrable commitment to widening access to higher education through a dispersed campus network and to using higher education as a powerful force for community regeneration.

All this sprang from the foundation of Christ Church as a Church of England training college in 1962, the first (and one of only two) to be established by the Church in the 20th century. Christ Church may have been the last of its type but the College was never content to stand still. It quickly expanded in response to government demands for more college-trained teachers and, when this policy was thrown into reverse in the early 1970s, adapted by building up a diversified range of courses based on its core strength in professional teacher training. This in turn led to an explosion of growth from the late 1980s when the College added courses in health and social care. In the late 1990s, with wider access to higher education a political priority, the College seized with relish the opportunity for further expansion, spreading its expertise to more distant parts of the county. By now, the reputation of the College for educational innovation, combined with its outward-looking nature, had also led to educational partnerships beyond Kent, not only in the UK but also overseas. As Christ Church became a University College in 1998, it was well on the way towards achieving full university status.

While the continuous evolution of Christ Church was inevitably influenced by external circumstances, this depended much more on the clear vision and drive of successive College Principals as well as the commitment of staff. Without this, the College may have closed

The Old Sessions House.

many years ago, the fate of so many other similar institutions during the 1970s. But this willingness to change has never compromised the Anglican ethos of Christ Church. The University today remains as warm and welcoming as it did as a College in the 1960s. The mix of students, in terms of their accomplishments or backgrounds, whether they are part-time or full-time, mature or coming straight from school, has always been diverse and Christ Church has consistently excelled at tapping into the often hidden potential of those who have come to study there.

The four chapters that follow focus on the development of key areas within the University while covering distinct phases in the University's history – the first on the origins and early growth of the College, the second on the pursuit of survival through diversification, the third on the expansion which stemmed from healthcare education, and the fourth on the path to university status in 2005. The aim is to show how the character of today's University has been shaped by its history and how those characteristics are constantly renewed and developed, propelling Christ Church forward in each succeeding generation.

Above: The chapel at night with Canterbury Cathedral in the background. The chapel is at the heart of the Canterbury campus.

Right: Canterbury Christ Church University has a student population of over 14,000 with campuses in the centre of Canterbury, Broadstairs, Medway, Tunbridge Wells (Salomons) and Folkestone.

Chapter One
Beginnings
1962–1976

ORIGINS

Christ Church College was born of two things – the traditional involvement, directly and indirectly, of the Church of England in the education of the nation; and the post-war development of teacher training.

The Church, through parish churches and charitable foundations, was linked with many of the earliest schools. The masters of most grammar schools were almost always ordained priests. Then the Church became involved in many of the hundreds of elementary schools that grew up in the 19th century to meet the educational needs of the expanding working class. That influence remains visible today in the many Church primary and secondary schools.

With the responsibility of teaching children came the duty to supply sufficient properly trained teachers. Many of the earliest teacher-training colleges had strong ties to the Church. In 1839, for instance, Chester Diocesan Training College was founded by a group of influential Anglicans; in 1841 a local church body set up St John's College, York; and the Church's main educational foundation established Whitelands College in Roehampton. Interestingly, all these colleges would later become universities in their own right or, as in the case of Whitelands, form part of a university.

The assumption by the state of the responsibility for education, including the training of teachers, began to erode the influence of voluntary organisations. By 1944, when the Butler Education Act transformed the English school system and the McNair Report advocated a major shake-up of teacher training, the Church of England had not founded a single teacher-training college since the end of the previous century.

After the war education expanded at all levels to meet the forecast growth in population. Just as new schools were built and old ones were

Previous page: 'A View of Canterbury' (1797), an aquatint by Francis Jukes after an engraving by Edward Dayes. The view is from where the campus stands today.

Right: View of the Cathedral from St Martin's Priory.

improved, and new universities were founded and older ones expanded, so new teacher-training colleges were started while existing ones were enlarged and refurbished. The incentives favoured state training colleges which increased from 28 in 1939 to 76 in 1951. The number of voluntary colleges, including those run by the Church of England, actually fell from 63 to 56 in the same period.

But the state soon realised that it could not on its own train enough new teachers for the rising school population. More than 70,000 primary-school classes still exceeded the recommended size of 40 pupils. In the late 1950s the government launched another expansion of teacher training and by June 1960 an extra 24,000 places had been authorised. Now the government was eager to involve the voluntary bodies who were allocated extra teacher-training places according to the number of pupils in their schools.

It was this which led to the foundation of Christ Church, Canterbury, the first Anglican training college since St Gabriel's in south London in 1899.

The McNair Report had fostered stronger links between the training colleges and the universities, with several founding institutes of education, but the colleges were widely seen just as providers of primary-school teachers. The government itself specified that the colleges should train 85 per cent of their students for primary education. Several colleges, including Christ Church, would overcome this barrier, in partnership with university institutes of education, by devising courses covering pupils from eight to 14 years of age.

In spring 1959 the Church Assembly approved the recommendation of the Church's Board of Education to build a new training college. Canterbury was chosen as the site, thanks in large part to the persuasive arguments employed by Canon Leonard Appleton, the diocesan director of education. Situated in the historic heart of the Anglican communion, the new college would fill a gap in the provision of teacher training in the south-east of England. It was hoped that the new college would also forge strong links with the new university expected to be established in the city. In the meantime, the college would seek advice and guidance from the University of London's Institute of Education (ULIE).

The first meeting of the new college steering committee took place in London on Thursday 22 October 1959. Under the chairmanship of Bishop Cockin of Bristol, this meeting of all the Church bodies concerned, as well as representatives of the Kent and Canterbury local education authorities, decided that the College should have a minimum number of 400 students, balanced between men and women, with an emphasis on secondary work, specialising in divinity,

Christ Church College was founded in 1962 to train teachers. Classes were originally held in St Martin's Priory. Shown here are the magnificent gardens of the Priory which are now a popular venue for conferences and the front of the Priory.

mathematics and science. Much of this had changed by the time the first students arrived in October 1962. Firstly, the College increased its minimum numbers from 400 to 500 in response to a further increase by the government in trainee teacher numbers. Secondly, specialisation in secondary teaching and in maths and science was abandoned. Most students sought training as primary-school teachers and too few wished to take up either maths or science. But these changes made little difference to the courses proposed by the College. The requirements laid down by ULIE provided one scheme for both primary and secondary students, combining teaching practice with the study of education and one main traditional subject. While relying on ULIE, the College was already making plans for its relationship

Dr Michael Ramsey, Archbishop of Canterbury, talking to a student at St Martin's Priory. In his address to the 75 new students he said, 'You are seeking freedom and truth, which is an exciting adventure. You are free to believe what you are convinced is true and refuse what you are convinced is untrue. All this freedom is yours.' (Kentish Gazette)

The first student registering at the College, left, helped by Dr Mason, the Principal, and Miss Young, the Vice Principal, 25 September 1962.

Mrs Wellard, one of the first teacher training students, 1962.

Frederic Mason, Principal, 1962–1975.

with the proposed University of Kent at Canterbury (UKC). It was hoped among other things that College students would be able to take their first degrees at UKC although the details remained unclear.

There was some indecision about the College's name. The final choice was left to the Bishop of Peterborough and the Archbishop of Canterbury. Their selection of Christ Church, echoing the dedication of the city's great cathedral, was confirmed in March 1961. There appears to have been no hesitation in naming the student halls of residence a couple of years later, all taking their names from Archbishops of Canterbury or suffragan bishops from the diocese – Fynden, Thorne, Davidson, Lang, Temple, Cockin and Fisher. The first five buildings still serve the same role today.

By the time the College had been named, the first Principal was already in post. There were a number of high-flying applicants for the job but Frederic Mason was not among those initially interviewed. He first appeared on the shortlist of three from which he was appointed on 31 May 1960. Aged 46, he came with a first-class degree in natural sciences from Cambridge, where he had also gained his Certificate of Education. After teaching, he lectured in education at Leeds University before being appointed as professor of education in the new University of Malaya in 1950. He built up from scratch the University's education department and was sent in 1957 to develop the University's new Kuala Lumpur campus. Known by generations of students as Dr Mason, his title came from the honorary doctorate he later received from the University. He was not ordained at the time of his appointment as Principal, taking holy orders the following year.

The chapel under construction.
(Kentish Gazette)

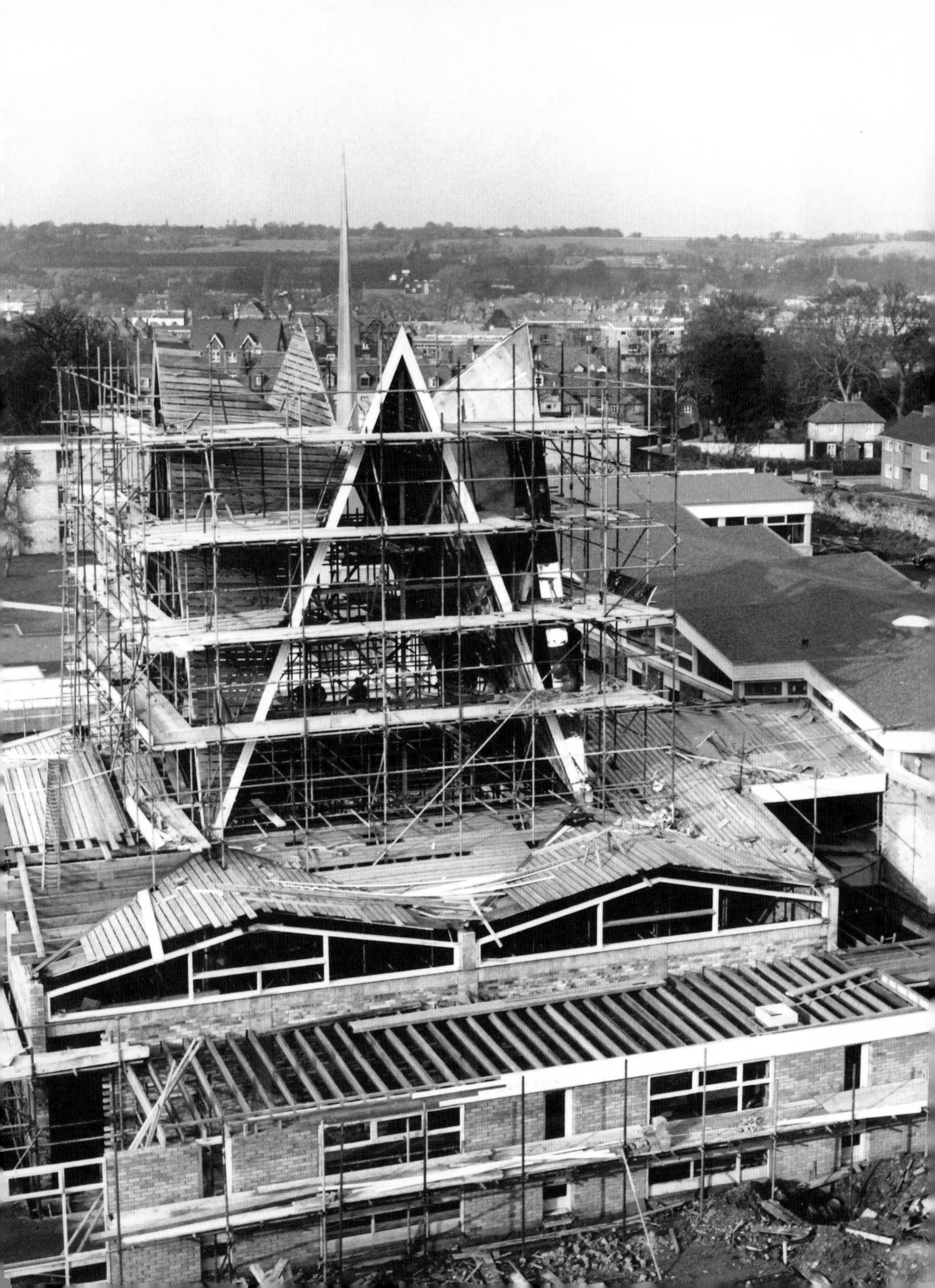

GREETINGS

712 GTG 10.20 EXETER T 28 GREETING =

PRINCIPAL STAFF AND STUDENTS OF CHRISTCHURCH COLLEGE CANTERBURY =

ALL BEST WISHES FOR TODAY AND FOR YOUR PATRONAL FESTIVAL ON FRIDAY =

PRINCIPAL STAFF AND STUDENTS STLUKES COLLEGE EXETER +

TELEGRAM

GREETINGS TELEGRAM

185 GTG 1.38 BRISTOL T 15 GREETING THE PRINCIPAL CHRISTCHURCH COLLEGE CANTERBURY

= WARMEST GREETINGS MAY YOUR COLLEGE PROSPER

COLLEGE OF STMATHIAS

+ + BS O E

GPO

Greetings telegrams sent to the College to celebrate its official opening, 1964.

A Christian ethos lay at the heart of Christ Church College. Outwardly this was evident from its name, from the placing of the proposed chapel at the heart of the new buildings and from the appointment of the Archbishop of Canterbury as Visitor to the College. More importantly, it was present from the very beginning in a commitment to a Christian outlook on teaching. When Bishop Cockin handed over the affairs of the College to the first chairman of the new governing body, the Archdeacon of Maidstone, the Very Reverend Gordon Strutt, the latter hoped that

> *the College would be a place where those who come may not only be trained in the technical business of teaching, but may find in their own fellowship in the College, and in chapel and in relations with the staff, a rich expression of Christian community living.*

Dr Mason told one journalist soon after the College opened in 1962 that

> *you must have a tremendous personal concern based on a sound understanding of human nature ... The College aims to send out teachers with a sound sense of purpose that can be passed on to the children and we think we cannot do this unless the whole basis is a Christian one.*

The dedication of the buildings, the consecration of the chapel and the official opening of the College did not take place until the autumn of 1964. The dedication by the Bishop of Maidstone took place within a communion service, followed by a College breakfast and a brief service in the hall when College representatives asked the Bishop to pray for those connected with Christ Church. 'Both services,' reported Dr Mason, 'were deeply moving and one felt that the College had been brought to the heart of the Christian religion.' The opening of the College was celebrated on 28 October by a service of thanksgiving in Canterbury Cathedral which was filled with staff, students, parents, parish and diocesan representatives, teachers and educationists.

The chapel today.

Environment

One reason for the delayed official opening was that the entire College campus was not supposed to be ready for occupation until September 1964. Students had been accepted prior to this date at the express request of the Ministry of Education. Temporary accommodation had to be found and St Martin's Priory, an old, rambling property dating largely from the sixteenth and seventeenth centuries, was purchased in 1961.

At the same time the College also paid £85,000 for the eight-acre site on which the campus was built. The largest part had belonged to the adjacent St Augustine's College, the Anglican missionary training college opened in 1848. St Augustine's stood on the site of the monastery of the same name, dissolved in 1538, and the campus appears to have formed part of the monastery grounds and gardens. After the dissolution the land was planted first with hops and later with fruit trees. The former almonry buildings became a brew-house, later owned by a fruit-packing business, and this was also acquired by the College in 1961.

The steering committee took the enlightened decision to organise an architectural competition for the College buildings. The winning £600,000 submission, announced in the summer of 1960, came from Robert Matthew & Johnson Marshall. Their design was said by the assessor to have 'achieved a sense of community', creating a focus on the chapel, with a sense of scale and intimacy, grouping buildings in quadrangles or cloisters, with ample free space around them. While today's University has long since outgrown the original Canterbury campus, the latter still retains an intimate feel. The buildings, while very much of their time, blend harmoniously with the well-tended gardens, green spaces and water features, the overall effect creating a sense of well-being. The campus has only one modest tower block

Building work on Christ Church campus, 1963. (Kentish Gazette)

Above: The campus was designed to 'achieve a sense of community' with buildings skilfully grouped in quadrangles and cloisters, surrounded by attractive open spaces that have been thoughtfully planted and cared for over the years.

Left: Students and staff looking at the building work, 1962.

and the rising gradient of the site along North Holmes Road presents wonderful views across to the majestic medieval cathedral.

A shortage of money prevented all the planned buildings from being built and the progress of the contractors was delayed by the appalling winter weather of 1963. So the first students to occupy the new buildings later that year found parts of the campus incomplete

and other parts being put to uses not originally intended. Nevertheless, by the autumn of 1964 the campus was finished, with its chapel, arts and education block, fine art, craft and design wing, geography, mathematics and science wing, music room, small gym and squash courts, tutors' rooms, student hostels, sick bay, library, hall and refectory. The arts and education block has become known as Hepworth, the geography, maths and science wing as Somerville and the fine art, craft and design wing was demolished as part of later extensions to the library.

Prior to the completion of the chapel, students used St Martin's Church, the oldest parish church in England. The cost of building the chapel, a striking design at the heart of the campus, actually left the College in debt which an appeal launched earlier in 1964 was intended to pay off. Raising money this way had been discussed on and off since before the College had been given the go-ahead, but in the end the appeal was badly organised and poorly received, raising just £14,000. The impressive curtain and screen in the chapel were commissioned by the College from David Holt, later Head of Art. The organ came from a London cinema in Leicester Square, donated by the cinema owners and carefully reassembled at the College.

Playing fields acquired at Stodmarsh Road were also ready for use by 1964, although the pavilion was not completed until 1966. As student numbers rose, a three-storey block, later known as Erasmus,

Top: Detail from the Chapel Screen.

Above: Life-size sketch of Christ which Holt drew when planning his tapestry.

Right: David Holt, former Head of Art, making the Chapel Screen, 1963–4.

Next page: The Chapel Screen, designed and made by David Holt depicting Christ in Majesty above the Tree of Life.

ISE SHINE FOR
THY LIGHT IS COME

LL DRAW ALL MEN UNTO ME

Above: Coleridge House.

Left: Students relaxing at the Canterbury campus.

designed by Robert Paine & Partners for lockers, seminar rooms and the Students' Union, was added in 1968. After it was completed, a thanksgiving service was held in the cathedral and attended by more than a thousand people.

The College never lacked ambition under Dr Mason or his successor, Michael Berry, who took over as Principal in 1975. In the late 1960s extensive plans drawn up for expanding the College had to be scaled down after the government began to cut back teacher-training numbers. But the College still acquired from St Augustine's College the last of the former almonry buildings, Coleridge House, in 1969, and what had become the Department for Education and Science (DES) approved new facilities for music, speech and drama. Coleridge House was used for study space and the new block, today forming an integral part of Powell, and also designed by Robert Paine & Partners, was occupied by the autumn of 1972.

In 1975, when it became clear that St Augustine's would close in the following year, Michael Berry immediately put forward proposals for Christ Church to take over the property. It was an opportunity, he said, for Christ Church to become 'a formidable Anglican college'. It soon became clear that the trustees of St Augustine's were more interested in leasing different parts of the site to different bodies. Both UKC and King's School, Canterbury, were also interested. Christ Church put forward a proposal to lease part of the site for more student accommodation and negotiations convinced the governing body that this would be accepted. Ultimately, the entire site was leased to King's School in 1976, but in acrimonious circumstances which prompted the Christ Church governors to pursue an unsuccessful appeal against the decision to the Charity Commissioners.

This was a major disappointment to the College, but despite an economic climate increasingly inhospitable to educational expansion the College authorities refused to be deterred from looking forward. Even while the negotiations with St Augustine's were under way, plans were also being made for a major extension to the original and now overcrowded library.

Erasmus.

Governing

As Frederic Mason later wrote, 'much of what took place in Christ Church College took place because it was the Principal's views'. While this applied just as much under his successor, Michael Berry, the governing body, particularly under the chairmanship of Geoffrey Templeman from 1965 onwards, also played a key role in the development of the College.

Paternal and avuncular towards his students, Dr Mason struggled to understand the social revolution taking place among the young. Deference was in decline as the age of majority was lowered to 18 and students demanded greater rights. Although discontent on the Christ Church campus was insignificant compared with the worst unrest among the universities, the strain of dealing with this change to the settled order was seen by some as contributing to Dr Mason's eventual decision to retire early in 1975.

His contribution towards the development of the College has perhaps been under-appreciated. For Mason, teaching was as much about knowledge as it was about teaching methods. Christ Church undoubtedly benefited from his strong belief that good teachers were educated teachers and educated teachers would only emerge if they were taught by well-qualified staff. For 12 years his deputy was Vivien Young, appointed from Whitelands College in 1961. Other members of the senior management team included the bursar, initially AR Knight and then after 1972 Jim Blanthorn, and, from 1965, the academic registrar, Tom Hetherington. From the very beginning of the College, academic affairs were placed in the hands of academic staff through the creation of an Academic Board which remains in place today.

Miss Young was succeeded in 1973 by Michael Berry. Educated at Durham, Oxford and Edinburgh

Dr Frank Fricker (English) and Reg Knight (Bursar), taking a break outside the library, 1967.

Staff picnic, 1965. From left, Mrs McCulloch, Peter McCulloch (Art and Poetry) and far right, looking at camera, Miss Young.

universities, with an honours degree in history, postgraduate certificate of education and a master's degree in education, he had been principal lecturer in education at St Peter's College, Saltley, before coming to Christ Church. He was a very different man from Frederic Mason and his vision would play a central part in the remarkable expansion of the College from the late 1970s onwards.

The College's trust deed stipulated that two-thirds of governors (and the Principal) should be members of the Church of England. The Archdeacon of Maidstone took the chair until his translation to the bishopric of Stockport in 1965. The Archbishop of Canterbury nominated as his successor Dr Geoffrey Templeman, the first Vice Chancellor of UKC, who also took over the role of chairman. Templeman had made his name as a university administrator as registrar at Birmingham and relished his role in building up a completely new university. Yet he still had the energy to be an active and interventionist chairman of the Christ Church governing body, a post he filled until his death in 1988 at the age of 74. A highly principled man, he was innately shy and diffident. He did not suffer fools gladly but those who stood up to him found him solicitous and supportive. This was particularly the case during the difficult years of the mid-1970s when teacher-training colleges nationally were rationalised. Christ Church's survival, and the close links it forged with UKC as a result of that, were due in part to Geoffrey Templeman.

LIVING

The College throughout this period was a small, intimate, friendly place. The Canterbury campus still retains these characteristics today. Although many students were living in lodgings spread throughout the city, most knew each other as they did most members of staff. The College, through the students, who were often found at various civic and community events, had an impact upon the city disproportionate to its size in the years before the University of Kent was properly established.

Most students had church connections of one sort or another. Places were hard to come by without a good reference from the parish priest. As members of an Anglican foundation, students formed close links between the College and the cathedral. Services were often held in the cathedral undercroft, students were regularly invited to attend tea parties held by the Dean and often acted as cathedral guides. Students expected to come together regularly for worship within the College. They set an example, complemented by many of the first members of staff, which remains an intrinsic element of Christ Church.

The College began at St Martin's Priory with 78 students – 51 women and 27 men, of whom ten were day students and 11 were aged over 25 – in September 1962. During their first week they were all addressed by the Archbishop, Michael Ramsey, who often made a habit of walking over to the College and chatting to students. There were always more women than men while primary-school teaching remained the focus of the College's activities.

With 227 students in the College, Dr Mason remarked to the governing body in December 1963 that 'it would take some time to establish community life in the College and to build up well-established traditions'. This was one reason why he introduced what

Lunch in the refectory, 1960s. (Kentish Gazette)

Left: Students in the common room, 1960s. (Kentish Gazette)

were known as the Triennial Celebrations, usually consisting of a thanksgiving service and other events held every three years, to reinforce among each generation of students an awareness of the origins and founding of the College.

He need not have worried about community life. Christ Church students from this period were eager pioneers. Sports teams were established – cricket, soccer and basketball for the men, netball and hockey for the women, and both sexes played tennis. Although the College had taken over existing squash courts on the site, there had never been any money to refurbish them and they were used as storage space for many years. Playing fields were acquired at Stodmarsh Road but they were not ready in time for the autumn term in 1964 so instead students used public playing fields and facilities kindly lent by local schools. Societies were formed and one of the earliest drama productions was *Edward II* in the cathedral chapter house. Plays were soon being performed on the outdoor stage in the main cloister on the campus. There were summer fairs and summer balls. The College refectory was used for dances and the bar in the Students' Union room for refreshments (soft drinks only). By the time Peter Jenkins took over as president of the Students' Union from Michael Wagg in 1963/64, student life appeared to be thriving. The list of societies ranged from debating and drama to French and jazz, from rambling and film to bell-ringing and a Campaign for Nuclear Disarmament group. There was a thriving College choir which sang regularly in the cathedral. The first rag week took place, getting somewhat out of hand when, in retaliation for the kidnapping by

Above: A scene from The Fire Raisers, *an early student drama production. (Kentish Gazette)*

A student in her new study bedroom.

Christ Church students of the Wye College mascot (a tortoise), Wye College students raided Christ Church at midnight, letting off as many fire extinguishers as they could find. (Wye College is an agricultural college 12 miles south of Canterbury.)

But students also began to look outwards. They took part in National Education Week, formed a Social Action Group, furthered links with community associations and schools, and organised weekend playgroups for local children. A dance raised funds for a local youth club, a party was arranged for the local children's home and a number of students visited patients in hospital. They were also able to look overseas. Several successful exchange visits were arranged with Elmira College in New York State during the late 1960s and early 1970s. A short-lived alumni association was formed in 1965 with the first reunion taking place in the following year.

In the summer of 1970, as numbers neared 700, Dr Mason noted that 'the record of the great majority of students is very good. One is moved by their friendliness and their sense of responsibility'. Students and staff worked closely together during these early years, both sides finding their feet in a new institution, cooperating in seeking to shape its future, and creating some long-lasting friendships in the process.

Left: Front cover of Clang, *published in 1968 by Christ Church to celebrate the past, present and future of colleges of education.*

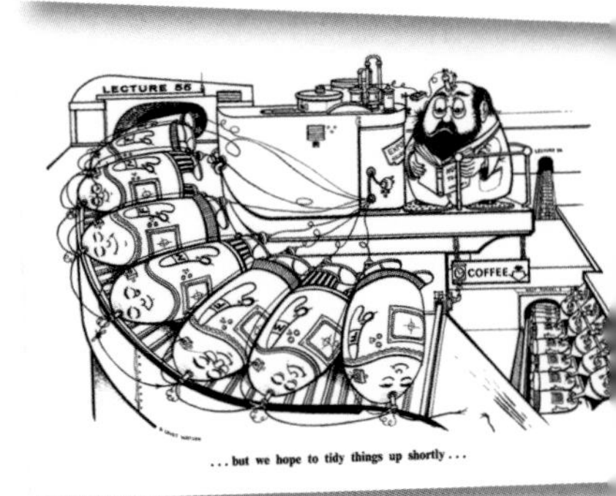

Cartoons from Clang, *1968.*

This was possible because the College was still small. The social life for staff and students was very good. There were staff outings such as the 'champagne picnics' to Sissinghurst with hampers filled with food by the catering department. And staff personally entertained the students in a way that would not be possible in later years.

On the other hand, the relationship between students, through the Students' Union, and the College authorities became rather more problematic. While the constitution of the Union was drafted in 1964, the Union was formally established by the governing body only in the following year. For students, a key issue at the time was persuading the governing body to release funds to which the Union was entitled, a matter not properly resolved until 1972. The Christ Church Union found that affiliation with the University of London was invaluable in providing student support.

Students were also beginning to press for a more liberal regulation of their college lives. When Shalley Lewis attended the College in 1963, women had to be in their hostel by 9.45 pm during the week and 10.45 pm at the weekends, after which time the doors were locked. One of the duties of the student president in an age before security patrols were employed was to check that these doors were indeed locked. The Vice Principal, Miss Young, was very strict, refusing women students consent to wear trousers. When some took to wearing long multi-coloured woollen stockings during the fierce winter of 1963, the immediate ban issued by Miss Young prompted sympathetic action from the staff the following morning, when two of them, Lorna Kendall and Mabel Whitaker, arrived in their own psychedelic leg-wear. Much of this approach stemmed from the position of the College authorities *in loco parentis* to young people whom the state did not regard as adults until they reached the age of 21. There was an atmosphere of benevolent paternalism, exemplified by the invitations to sherry every Sunday evening from the Principal to the three personal tutors and their students. On the campus there was a resident matron and housekeeper, Miss Russell, who was also warden of the women's hostel. Miss Tyler was the resident tutor. There were also several other resident staff but it was becoming increasingly difficult to recruit staff prepared to take on residential duties. It was also proving difficult for those in these positions who had been in teaching for many years to respond to the shifting social attitudes of the 1960s. Ultimately, there was a change in the law to lower the age of majority to 18 which came into force on 1 January 1970.

Paternalism governed not just the regulation of student life within Christ Church, as in many other places of higher education. It was also evident in the way the authorities neglected to take into account student opinion in the way the College was run. Geoffrey Templeman warned his fellow governors in 1968 that the unrest seen in universities and colleges across the country was likely to spread to Christ Church. There was friction within the College but on nothing like the scale seen elsewhere. Dr Mason dragged his feet in response to pressure from the Union for the reform of rules and regulations, the appointment of a sabbatical president and the opening of the Union bar on Sundays. Everything came to a head during 1971. Fed up with the procrastination of the Principal, students decided to boycott the College celebrations planned for the summer and stage a sit-in. Matters were only resolved when Dr Templeman stepped in. The Principal was sidelined and his responsibilities for student matters were delegated to the College's Academic Board. Approval was quickly forthcoming for Sunday bar opening and the post of a sabbatical union president. But the governing body resisted student representation until the end of 1973 when, despite vocal opposition, it was agreed by a vote of 9–4 that there should be two student governors.

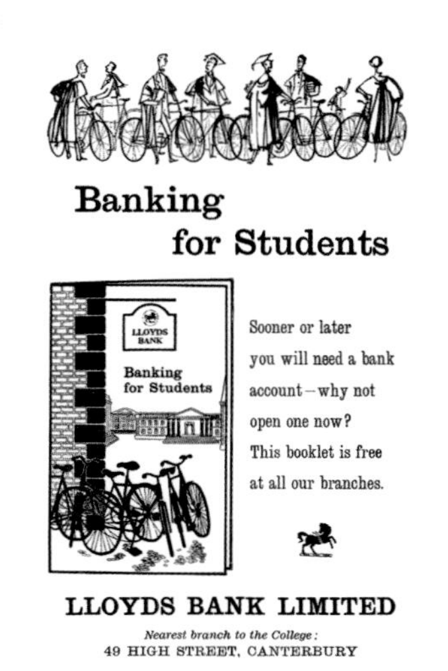

Lloyds Bank advertisement, 1964.

That was also the year when the celebrated case of Herring vs Templeman was finally resolved. A student had been dismissed from the College but claimed he had been denied natural justice. The court held that his appeal failed on every count, regarding the way the case had been handled by the governing body as exemplary, a tribute to the administrative expertise of the chairman. The governing body's Working Party on Moral Issues Affecting Students had regretfully concluded only the year before that they had to accept the much more limited grounds on which a student could be excluded from training as a teacher proposed by the DES, after Dr Mason had 'outlined the great changes which had taken place in the public mind with regard to its attitude to extra-marital sex, pregnancy and abortion'.

Nevertheless, the turmoil of the early 1970s soon subsided and in the summer of 1974 the Principal could remark once again that 'student life appears to proceed quietly'.

An advertisement for Martins Bank.

LEARNING

With Frederic Mason's conviction that knowledge was the key to good teaching, the most distinctive feature of the course was what Mason initially entitled Civilisation, later Combined Studies and ultimately Contemporary Studies. Similar in range to the inter-disciplinary studies being taught in universities, nothing like it was being taught in any other Anglican teacher-training college. The course required the involvement of every department (although under Mason, averse to the title because of his experience of inter-departmental rivalry, departments were known as fields of study), but many departmental heads regarded Contemporary Studies as ill-defined and a hindrance to the in-depth teaching of their own subjects. Nor was the course popular with students who felt it deprived them of a second curriculum main course as practised at most other colleges. Peter Jenkins, the second president of the Students' Union, recalled 'completing a whole term on the rituals associated with the tribes of the former Gold Coast and thinking the whole exercise was a waste of time!'

Peter Jenkins, the second President of the Students' Union, 1963. (Kentish Gazette)

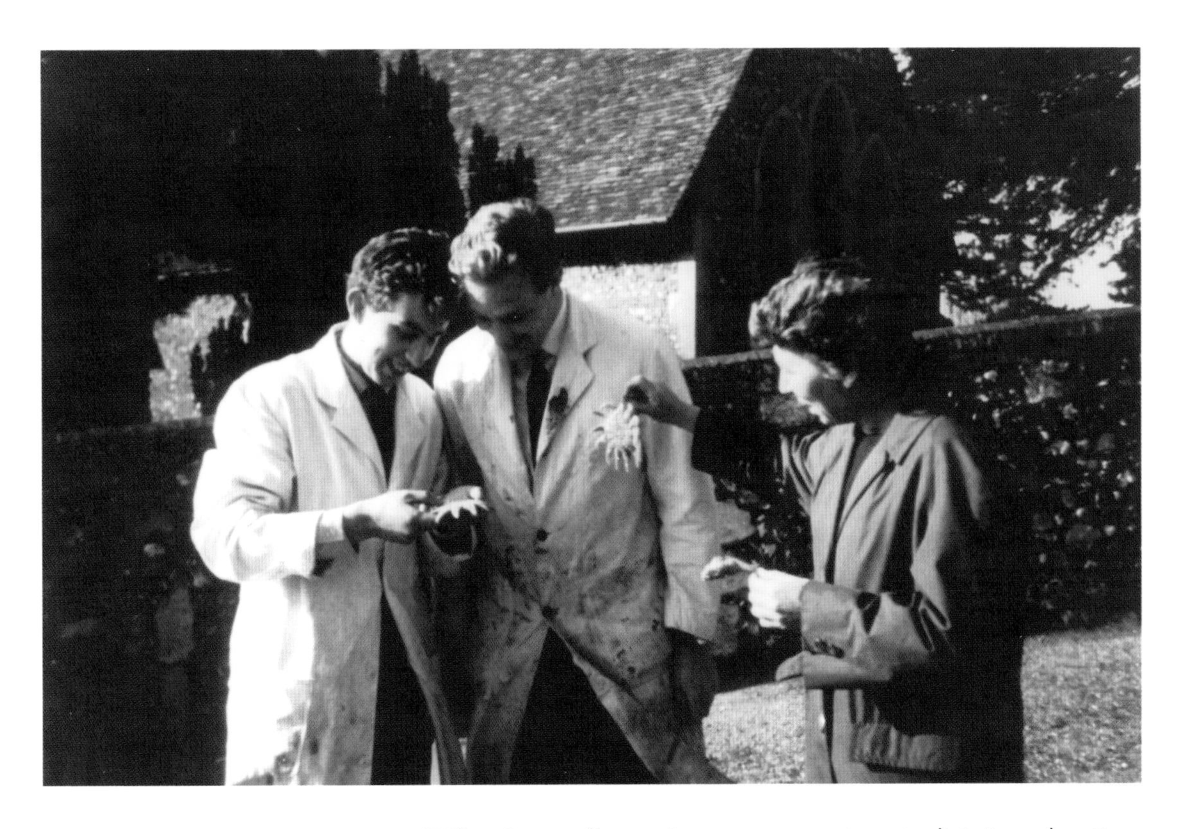

Mabel Whitaker, Head of Science, with students outside the Priory, 1963.

The first staff appointments were in art, divinity, education, geography, science, mathematics and English. Appointments in music and craft eventually followed. Mason later outlined the basis of his appointments. 'I was asked to aim at university standards and my professional experience had been in a university department of education where the majority of lecturers had been appointed because of their experience in teaching particular subjects.' He was seeking well-qualified staff with practical experience of teaching. Those first appointments in December 1961 set the standard for the College – H Armstrong-Jones (education), AL Flight (maths), James Gibson (English), Lorna Kendall (divinity), WJ Kirkham (physical sciences) and Mabel Whitaker (biological sciences). Gibson, for instance, urbane, courteous and tolerant, came from Dulwich College with a reputation as a Hardy scholar and worked well with students. Lorna Kendall, excitable, slightly eccentric, with a complete disregard for time, had an international reputation as a scholar and was well-connected within the Church, counting Michael Ramsey as a great friend. Clear and incisive, Alf Flight's strengths encompassed not only modern maths but also music and he ran the College choir. Kirkham, young and handsome, strongly evangelical, a knowledgeable and effective teacher, was the College pin-up among women students. Mabel Whitaker, a small, busy, widely read and deeply religious woman with a zest for life and a sense of fun, enthused her students.

HM Queen Elizabeth during a visit to the College, 1965. (Kentish Express)

She took them off on expeditions to investigate differing habitats so they might understand how in the world outside the classroom all the sciences came together. These expeditions were challenging, exciting and sometimes dangerous – one student remembers how collecting plankton off Whitstable almost cost him his life. All but one of these first members of staff came from school teaching and Mason, sensitive to the criticism that staff in many colleges lacked teaching experience, believed this was vital in training new teachers. The exception was Armstrong-Jones. He stayed only a short time but most of the rest stayed with the College for several years. The last member of staff to join the College was the librarian, Tony Edwards. He arrived only two weeks before the beginning of term. The delay in his appointment came because Mason was keen to appoint a professional librarian rather than an academic who would look after the library and he had had to fight his corner with the Ministry of Education.

In the 1960s the entrance requirements for teacher-training colleges, or colleges of education as they became known in 1964, were not high. Only 37 per cent of Christ Church's intake in the autumn of 1963 came with two or more 'A' levels. Ten years later the percentage was scarcely any higher. It was only in 1976, following the James Report, that this became the minimum requirement for every new student. But the College's pass rates for the teaching qualification, the Certificate of Education, were high, never less than 90 per cent and sometimes in excess of 95 per cent. The Certificate was eventually superseded by higher qualifications. The degree of Bachelor of Education (BEd) was introduced in 1968 (Norman Watson was the College's first first-class BEd graduate in 1970) and the Post-Graduate Certificate of Education (PGCE) in 1971. Mason welcomed

Lunch in the dining room, 1960s.

Students singing in the chapel, 1970.

the new degree, believing it would 'give long-needed educational recognition to a section of students in Colleges of Education'. To introduce the BEd, the College once again had to meet the requirements of ULIE. The latter had never been happy with Contemporary Studies and accepted a revised form of the course with some reluctance. Staff, on the other hand, felt that ULIE was placing unnecessary obstacles in the path of those students wishing to progress from the Certificate of Education to the BEd. As a result, the College's Academic Board contacted UKC in 1968 to discover whether or not those students who did well in the Certificate could undertake part two of a first degree within UKC. There had already been an approach from UKC in the previous year, seeking the College's involvement in UKC's proposed Delegacy in Teacher Training. UKC also offered the College the opportunity for students to work towards a first degree and for staff to work towards higher degrees. This was the beginning of closer links which would eventually see UKC take over from ULIE as the validating authority for the College's courses.

The BEd and PGCE formed part of government plans to carry on expanding teacher training while raising standards. In the late 1960s the College had grown to 720 students and was once again overcrowded. Initially Christ Church as a relatively unknown college was rarely the first choice of many applicants. Tom Hetherington, the registrar, with a small group of staff, tackled this by advertising the College, attending careers evenings in Kent schools and colleges, talking to sixth forms, inviting interested mature students to attend advisory interviews and building links with Kent County Council's careers service. This steadily paid off for the College always filled the places it had available.

The Principal was eager to capitalise on government willingness to fund more teacher-training places. He wanted to increase College numbers to 1,100. From the time of his appointment, he had taken every opportunity to press the case for expanding numbers, sometimes in the face of considerable reluctance from the governing body. This time his ambition failed because the government abandoned their original plans in favour of more limited expansion, having discovered that recruitment had exceeded expectations. But he still succeeded in securing additional accommodation to alleviate the College's overcrowding.

A science experiment, 1970.

In response to growing concern about standards, the government commissioned a wider investigation into the future of teacher training under Lord James of Rusholme, the Vice Chancellor of York University. The entrance requirement for Christ Church students may have been relatively low but examination results showed the College had enabled the great majority of them to reach their potential. For the years 1972–74, for example, all 69 BEd candidates graduated, six with upper seconds and two with firsts; while there was a success rate of 94 per cent among PGCE candidates and 96 per cent among those studying for the Certificate of Education. Another complaint levelled against education colleges was the lack of practical experience among their staff. This, Frederic Mason pointed out to governors, certainly did not apply to Christ Church. He was still making appointments in the same way as he had when the College was first opened. Sean Greenwood, for instance, came from a secondary school to Christ Church in 1974 to teach history to student teachers. His MA, he recalled, was regarded as a cut above most people's qualifications.

It was clear even before the James Report was issued in 1972 that, with too many new teachers being produced, the future of many teacher-training colleges was at stake. The governing body in July 1970 heard Dr Mason sum up the situation. It was important that the College should continue to carry out the professional training of teachers but, given the current surplus and the opportunities to obtain teaching qualifications elsewhere, it was also clear that the College should develop a role in higher education encompassing additional subject areas. At the same time the chairman, Geoffrey Templeman, voiced his concern that if the training colleges took up the liberal arts, they would attract the least able candidates, lose their vocational character and exacerbate graduate unemployment. In every respect he was to be proved wrong.

The James Report forecast a continuing need for more teachers, just not as many as the government had previously been predicting. Many of the training colleges established during the 1960s faced closure. Between 1975 and 1985 the number of colleges training teachers would fall, largely through merger or amalgamation, from 168 to 20. The Report also suggested that voluntary colleges should train only half their students as teachers. The immediate consequence was that half of all training colleges were closed. Christ Church faced a battle for survival. It had to raise standards, widen its intake and introduce new subjects, all in a very short space of time. As the governing body minutes recorded during a debate on the future of the College in the summer of 1973, 'the College needed to find other work to do if it was not to be substantially reduced in size'. On the basis of the White Paper which followed the James Report, it was

Sport science – dancers holding a dramatic pose, 1970s.

reckoned that Christ Church would be reduced to 500 students in total by 1980. It did not help that in the spring of 1974 the DES slashed recruitment to Christ Church by almost a third, considerably more than the average decrease for colleges in the south-east of England. At the same time other institutions, notably the polytechnics, were competing for the same students who had once been attracted to the colleges of education and there was also less demand for teaching places.

Closure was not the only threat to the College. Many colleges were seeking integration or absorption with other institutions. The Christ Church governors were determined that the College should remain an independent Anglican college. While it seemed evident that stronger links should be developed with UKC, the idea of becoming an integral part of the university, which had already tried and failed to absorb Wye College, was discussed only briefly. And in its ambition to remain independent Christ Church received strong backing from the local education authority. The support of Kent County Council, which looked to Christ Church to supply many of its teachers, came at the expense of closing one of its own colleges at Sittingbourne. Students from Christ Church were well-known in Kent's schools, taking their teaching practice in schools from Canterbury, Deal, Dover and Folkestone to Maidstone, Ashford, Gillingham, Hythe and Sittingbourne.

The plans for the survival and transformation of the College were developed during 1973–75. ULIE was interested only in the education of teachers so the plans envisaged a much closer relationship with UKC through the validation by the latter of the

Sport science students today.

Above left: Teacher training today.

Above right: Trainee teachers taking part in a discussion group, 1974.

College's teaching qualifications and proposed new joint degree courses established in association with the University. It was expected that new courses would have to cater for a quarter of the College's students by 1980. Staff were clear that these courses must for the most part build on the College's existing strengths; but it was obvious that more diverse courses should also be offered. Among the subjects considered were educational psychology, social work, teaching English as a foreign language (TEFL) and paramedical training on behalf of the regional health authority. The recruitment of overseas students was also discussed.

There was a hitch in achieving these aims. The governors hoped that ULIE would continue to validate the College's courses until an agreement had been reached with UKC. Instead, ULIE rejected this request. The stumbling block once more was the Contemporary Studies component of the BEd. ULIE agreed to continue as the validating authority but ultimately Contemporary Studies had to be jettisoned.

In September 1975 the College was relieved to hear that the DES had agreed Christ Church could continue as an independent college of education. The Department had accepted the College's proposal that 'it should remain mono-technic with a limited degree of diversification'. Geoffrey Templeman was not complacent. He pointed out that Christ Church would be one of only four 'essentially teacher-training and free-standing church colleges left ... in these circumstances it was important for the College to serve the Church by aiming for excellence and to be a place worth coming to'.

Frederic Mason, worn out from the stresses of dealing with student demands and the anxiety of fighting for the future of the College he had started, retired early at the end of August 1975. The burden of securing the survival of the College was handed over to the new Principal, Michael Berry. In later years he would reflect, with considerable understatement, that 'it was not an easy time'.

Chapter Two
Diversification
1977–1989

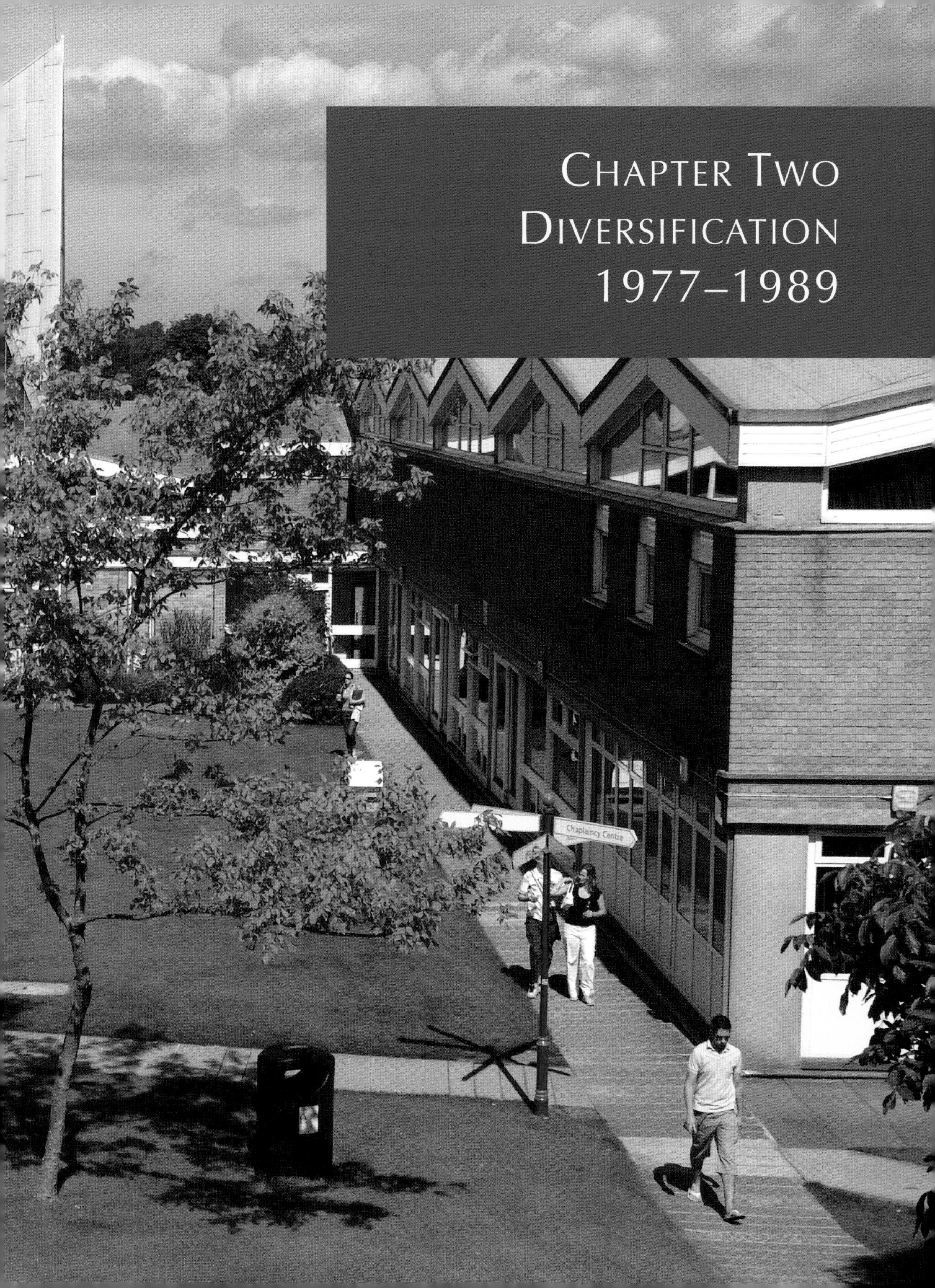

New Approach

Taking over where his predecessor had left off, Michael Berry began to put into place every necessary piece of the jigsaw needed to save the College. Early in 1976 departments were created for arts and sciences, diversified courses and interdisciplinary studies, educational studies and professional studies. The head of the latter was Dr Graham Brown, later appointed Vice Principal, and, with his visible energy and dynamism, the perfect foil for the Principal. The Berry–Brown duo would drive the College forward with an entrepreneurial zeal rarely seen in the field of higher education at that time. Berry was convinced that diversification would herald the expansion of the College. In the middle of 1976 the Niblett Report on the Church's Colleges of Higher Education was released. Its recommendations chimed with Christ Church's intentions – developing degrees other than the BEd, specialising in the range of careers for which diversified courses were offered, developing strong links with other educational institutions and businesses, and ensuring staff were competent to deliver the new courses.

Professor Grenville Hancox, Head of Music, accompanying a violin student. The Department of Music is acknowledged widely to be one of the most active and exciting centres for the composition, production, performance and study of music in the South East.

YAMAHA

Music students.

A key part of this strategy involved closer links with UKC. The transfer from ULIE to UKC as the College's validating authority was a complex process but it was finally agreed that UKC would take over from September 1978. In the meantime, the first non-teaching degree, a BA in English and Religious Studies, was introduced under the aegis of ULIE. It began with five students in October 1976. In the same year, the College also introduced the first course offered jointly with UKC, a part-time MSc in physics and education.

The time taken to negotiate a change in validating authority left the College outside the time limit set by the DES for introducing new courses. Retrospective approval for these had to be sought, which came in October 1978. Throughout this period the College received great help from Maurice Vile, UKC's Pro-Vice Chancellor, who did much to accelerate both progress towards the delivery of joint courses and the agreement with UKC as the College's new validating authority. When the transfer from ULIE to UKC finally took place, he also speedily confirmed validation of the College's courses although this was on the understanding that they would be revalidated within a reasonable period of time. A review would also take place after three years to ensure that College staff had achieved the qualifications commensurate with teaching degree courses. UKC would also be involved in all academic appointments. Final links with ULIE were severed in 1981 as the last students on ULIE-validated courses left the College. On 21 November that year the first degrees awarded through UKC – one MA, 26 BAs, four BScs and 40 BEds – were conferred on Christ Church students at a degree ceremony in Canterbury Cathedral. It was a proud day for the College.

The first degrees derived from the content of the courses taught for the BEd, several of them from Combined Studies, although initially confined to English and Religious Studies. But the College also needed to develop completely new non-teaching-related courses. The problem was that Christ Church had concentrated for so long on training primary teachers that it was seriously short of other resources. This was where Berry's entrepreneurial opportunism came into play. On the closure in 1980 of Stockwell College in south London, he managed to secure for Christ Church all Stockwell's film and television equipment. With this, Christ Church could offer its first entirely new non-teaching course, in radio, film and television (RFTV) studies. Christ Church also acquired from Stockwell valuable resources for the development of art and music. All this was vital for the diversification needed to recruit 300 extra students and secure the College's survival.

Another innovation was the introduction in 1976 of a TEFL diploma and the creation of a language school for overseas students.

Christ Church has a strong tradition of welcoming students from abroad. The present international community of students is drawn from over 60 countries.

The College welcomed students from around the world, from countries such as the USA, the Netherlands and Romania. Links with Malaysia began around 1980, with the country sending a party of students to the College every year for a specially designed BEd course. By the end of the decade, the International Programmes Office established by the College offered more than English language courses. There were also courses for overseas teachers of English, links with European universities were being established for tourism and business studies courses and study programmes were being devised for students from US universities.

But in the late 1970s and early 1980s the process of diversification was in its infancy. In 1979 the new joint arts and science degrees accounted for only 20 per cent of a record intake for the College. It was the expansion of teacher training which gave the College the breathing space needed to develop other courses. This was achieved in spite of adverse circumstances that would have induced many college principals to throw up their hands in despair. The government squeeze on teacher training lasted well into the 1980s. Nationally the number of applicants fell sharply in the face of such uncertainty. Unemployment rates among newly qualified teachers were high. Yet the College always succeeded in filling its quota of teacher-training places. It also seized the chance to attract existing teachers back to the College either for in-service training (INSET) courses or, as part of the drive towards an all-graduate profession, for the BEd. Alongside the BEd and PGCE, Christ Church offered a wide range of degrees, diplomas and certificates aimed at serving teachers. Michael Berry placed Graham Brown in charge of teacher education and INSET and together they achieved considerable success in building up numbers and developing INSET resource centres within the College. Of the almost 400 students who joined the College in 1979, 168 were embarking upon education degrees and 128 on INSET courses. In 1984, when government inspectors reported on initial teacher training at Christ Church, they noted in particular how the wide range of courses 'illustrate the college's substantial commitment to the in-service education of teachers in the area' and commended the contribution made by the nine resource centres established in conjunction with the local education authority.

Media department.

Under Graham Brown and later Margaret Alfrey, who joined the College in 1983 from primary teaching, later becoming head of the department, teacher training remained one of the core strengths of the College. The reputation developed by Christ Church in this field led to invitations to monitor educational initiatives in several local education authorities and even to an increased allocation of teacher-training places in the late 1980s. An increase of 20 per cent was awarded on the grounds of the quality and reputation of the training provided by the College, its track record on meeting recruitment targets and its position as the sole local provider of both teacher training and INSET. The College also developed a close working relationship with the local education authority and successive county education officers.

There were other spin-offs from this. At the end of the 1980s the College's growing reputation attracted funding for new degrees in tourism, business studies and information technology, areas usually the preserve of the polytechnics. In turn, this continued growth in new areas balanced the eventual decline in INSET as it moved into the schools. On the other hand, in 1989 there was still only one English programme, the joint honours BA/BSc.

In 1980 the College established a health education resource centre for the Canterbury and Thanet District Health Authority. Several years later, the Department of Health and Social Security was searching for a partner in the south-east outside London to create a course in occupational therapy. Originally the choice was another college, Nonington, which specialised in physical education. When Nonington fell victim to education cutbacks, Michael Berry and Graham Brown took advantage of another opportunity. The DHSS came to Christ Church. Similar initiatives had been started in colleges elsewhere in the country to cater for a chronic shortage in the profession. Christ Church went one better. The three-year professional diploma, beginning in September 1987, validated by UKC and

Dance in chapel, early 1980s.

accepted by the professional body, would, with an extra fourth year, lead to a degree, the first of its kind in the UK. Michael Berry remarked that this 'could be regarded as an opportunity to make a significant extension to the professional work of the College in an area of evident national need'. This proved to be an understatement. The success of occupational therapy led to the introduction of a radiography course. The trend towards professional paramedical training was hugely important for the development of the College.

By 1988 Christ Church, once predicted to be on the verge of closure and expected to shrink to just 500 teaching students by 1980, was offering a broad range of courses to a diverse student body that now stood at more than 1,500. This was an astonishing turnaround, a tribute not only to the hard work and determination of Michael Berry but also to the commitment of his colleagues. Staff had risen to the challenge of moving from teacher training towards the delivery of non-teaching-related degrees and other qualifications.

Berry's aim had been to accomplish this with as few redundancies as possible. Between 1975 and 1981, with the redeployment of staff on new courses and their encouragement to achieve more advanced qualifications, there had been only two redundancies and those had been voluntary. In 1984, when the inspectorate reviewed the BA/BSc in Combined Studies, they found that almost all the staff involved had second degrees and a quarter had doctorates. Staff were delivering papers at conferences and publishing their research. All this had a knock-on effect on teacher training too, whose improvement reported on by a different team of inspectors in the same year was partly attributed to better qualified staff. In 1988 the College received national coverage when it acquired major funds for a research project into HIV/AIDS Education and Young People under Dr Stephen Clift and David Stears.

After School Club.

Admission requirements edged higher during this period but the College had not been founded to train an educational elite. It provided academic and professional training opportunities for many students of different attainments, ages and backgrounds. After the early days of diversified courses, when there had been a need for variable admission criteria, it was necessary to improve levels of attainment in several areas. But the College's reputation for teacher training attracted very well-qualified graduates for PGCEs while the proportion of upper second degrees steadily increased during the 1980s. Christ Church's strength lay in taking a wide range of students, enabling them to further their personal development and guiding them through to a worthwhile qualification, either academically or professionally.

The direction taken by the College under Michael Berry was very much in line with the views of the Church of England Board of Education. Perhaps a little late in the day, there was a recognition that Church colleges were vulnerable in an era when the links between church and state had become much looser. Considering the future of its colleges in 1985, the Church had recognised a decade later than Michael Berry that to survive they had to become much more distinctive, improving in particular the quality of their research and postgraduate study. Perhaps the most important conclusion the Board reached was that the Church should reaffirm its commitment to the colleges and restate its belief in the importance of the Church in state education.

Confident in the ability of better-qualified staff to teach university-validated degrees, Michael Berry and his deputy, Graham Brown, saw no reason why the College should not also offer research degrees. At this suggestion, recalled Brown, 'everyone fell off their chairs'. But the proposal to introduce research degrees, supported by Maurice Vile at UKC, was approved by the DES much more quickly than anyone expected. The proposal apparently perplexed the senior civil servant dealing with the matter so he asked his minister, Sir Keith Joseph, Secretary of State for Education, whether the request should be granted. Joseph, ever a man with an open mind, apparently said, 'Why not?' In 1983 Christ Church became the first college of higher education to offer PhD and MPhil degrees. Although they were few in number, part-time (the first one took eight years to complete) and with limited funding, they did serve to boost the College's academic profile, stimulate existing staff and help to attract well-qualified new staff. A sign of the College's improving academic quality came in 1985 when for the first time two Research Councils made awards to two postgraduate students at Christ Church.

In 1987 Michael Berry asked the governing body to note, in relation to the work done in the College, 'both the range and level of work now being undertaken, and stressed the importance of the solid core of professional training around which so much of it was based'. The move towards a wider view of professional training other than teaching had brought the College increased numbers and a boost to its finances. This was not simply because there were now so many more students at Christ Church. It was because these new ventures brought income to the College from sources other than the DES. The non-teaching degrees, for instance, were largely funded by the National Advisory Body for Public Sector Education (NAB) and came with far fewer restrictions than direct funding from the DES. Occupational therapy was financed by the DHSS and nursing training by the National Health Service (NHS). These new revenue streams made all the difference, particularly because surpluses could be reinvested into the College at a time when the DES expected voluntary colleges to find a quarter of the cost for all new buildings.

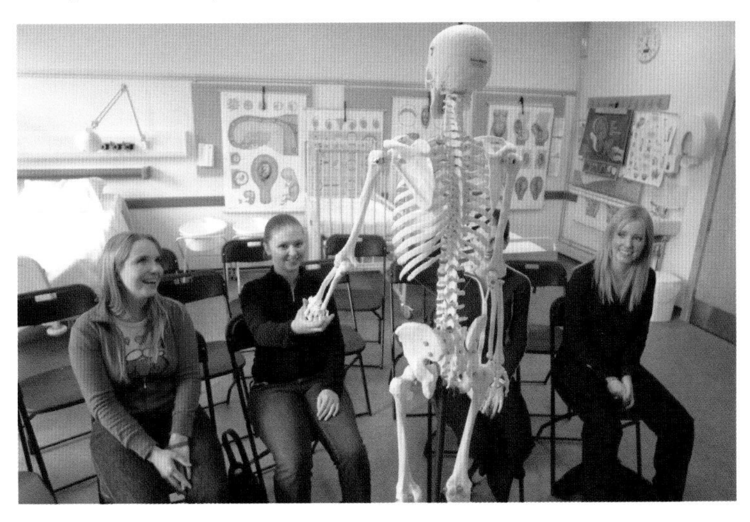

Health and Social Care students in a fully-equipped ward that forms part of the Skills Laboratory at the Medway Campus.

Environment

Diversification would change the face of the Canterbury campus. Initially, however, the College could scarcely find the money to make any physical improvements. This did not deter Michael Berry. With an eye for an opportunity, he spotted the potential of a nearby church. St Gregory's was the first church designed by Sir Giles Gilbert Scott. Built in 1848, it was declared redundant in 1978. Acquired by the College in 1981, it was partially converted in 1983 and reopened as a performing arts centre, although work was not completed until 1986. The conversion was funded through the Manpower Services Commission, a government body which provided employment for skilled workers who would otherwise have been out of a job. It was a typically entrepreneurial move from the College Principal.

MAMBO.

On the campus itself government cutbacks delayed one long-planned project. Students had never enjoyed adequate facilities. Now there were even more of them, providing a dedicated Students' Union building became even more urgent. First proposed in 1979, the £600,000 building was not completed until early 1985 but proved an immediate success.

The Union was just one part of an overall development plan for the campus drawn up in 1979 by David Coupe, from the Canterbury practice of Pateman and Coupe. The practice had first been involved

Previous page right: St Gregory's, acquired by the College in 1981, and now a performing arts centre.

Previous page left: Restoration work at St Gregory's, 1984.

Left: Canterbury campus from the top of the then Education block, 1988.

Below: The new Students' Union building and students in the bar, 1987.

in designing the extension to the College library in 1977. The development plan, of course, assumed future expansion, a risky prediction to make at a time when some considered the survival of the College was still at stake. Michael Berry, however, had another, more positive, vision. The plan took into account the need to retain views of the cathedral, sustain the quadrangle concept as well as the existing scale of the buildings, their relationship to each other and to the campus grounds, and provide decent landscaping. About the same time Coleridge House was turned into the music department. But, despite an often ingenious use of space, the campus could hardly cope with rising numbers of students. By now, however, the College was able to reap the financial benefits from its new courses. One of the first fruits was the long-planned Information Technology building, finally opened in 1987, and now known as Invicta. No sooner had this been brought into use than planning began for the first paramedical building, intended for occupational therapy and later called the Johnson Building. This first phase was funded entirely by grant-aid at a cost of £1.5 million; it was a sign of things to come.

Top: View of the library, today.

Bottom: Inside the Library.

Next page: The Students' Union at Canterbury today.

church

Living

The campus could not hope to accommodate the growing number of students coming to Christ Church during the 1980s. In 1983 the College provided only 230 residential places so most spent at least two years living out. The Students' Union Handbook from the time listed the minimum basic entitlements students should seek from lodgings – at least two baths a week, breakfast, 'a milk drink at night', a well-lit bedroom and somewhere reasonable to work, 'somewhere to wash and dry underwear and small articles of clothing' and a key to the door. 'The provision of these', continued the Handbook, 'depends on the disposition of the individual landlady, some of whom can be extremely mean'. By the end of the decade, suitable housing was becoming scarcer and rents much higher. This coincided with a reduction in student grants and benefit entitlements. On the campus itself, rising charges for student accommodation came with fewer facilities, such as those for drying and cooking.

The Students' Union began to play a greater role in College life as welfare and other issues became more important. On the other hand, the Union sometimes struggled to engage the interest of more than a handful of students in its affairs. But students during the 1980s needed little persuasion to take to the city's streets. This was the era of savage education cutbacks, unpopular education reforms and the community charge, more popularly known as the poll tax. In Canterbury, Christ Church students joined forces with their peers from

A student in her study bedroom, 1988.

Don't Quit

Left: Students on campus, 1980s.

Below: Inside the Students' Union, late 1980s.

Bottom: Tunisians on a TEFL course at the College, 1983. (Kentish Gazette)

UKC for mass street protests. With the erosion of grants and talk of top-up fees, students also had an ally in the College's governing body, which feared 'the creation of a credit dependency in students'. It was in general a time when relationships between students and the College authorities were much more settled, when there was even perhaps a sense of common purpose, with both sides united in tackling the impact of government decisions on the quality of College life.

This was also a period when the student body became much more diverse. There were more mature students, more students who were married or with families. A playgroup was already looking after the young children of students by the early 1980s. International students were also more evident at Christ Church. In 1983, for instance, the College hosted Tunisian students taking an English course, visitors from Elmira College, Russian trainee teachers and BEd students from Malaysia. Two years later the College fielded a soccer team which included players from Malaysia, Malawi, Tunisia, Japan, Cameroon, Switzerland, France and the UK.

All College activities benefited from a larger student body. Sport flourished as student teams of

both sexes took part in local leagues and the British Colleges Sports Association competitions. The choice was extensive, ranging from cricket, rugby and hockey to badminton, basketball, netball, tennis, squash, sailing and riding. The College began to chalk up a series of successes. In 1987, for instance, the soccer team reached the final of the Inter-Collegiate Cup, only to lose 2–1 to Trinity and All Saints, and won the local league challenge trophy. College societies multiplied, covering every activity from handbells, trampolining and tap dancing to CND and Amnesty International, enthusiasm waxing and waning with cyclical regularity. A fresher wrote in 1987 how

> *many of us arrived bright-eyed and bushy-tailed. We were eager beavers ready for the big adventure called Higher Education ... By the end of the first week, we had all-out enthusiasm squeezed out of us by the most stupefying apathy that hangs thick in the air. Initial numbers at the sports and societies fair have not been echoed at subsequent meetings.*

Above: The Winter's Tale, *1984.*

Right: The Taming of the Shrew, *1985.*

Above: Cover of theatre programme, 1984.

Left: Romeo and Juliet *on the outdoor stage adjacent to the pond, 1980s. (Kentish Gazette)*

The Students' Union did its best to blow away apathetic cobwebs by organising ever more exciting entertainments. In the autumn term of 1988, these included bands and discos, a fancy dress party, a fireworks night, a cabaret night, a folk night and the President's Ball. Budding DJs had their chance through the College radio station, set up in 1983. Eventually broadcasting for the best part of every day, seven days a week, it was called C4, taking its name from the acronym for Christ Church College Canterbury.

Art exhibition in St Gregory's, 1984.

Drama and music prospered. Plays ranged from Shakespeare and Wilde to Priestley, Ayckbourn and Thornton Wilder. Music became an inextricable part of life at Christ Church. A driving force behind much of this was Grenville Hancox, who came to lecture in music at the College in 1982, becoming head of department in 1988. The choir continued to sing in Canterbury Cathedral and received invitations to sing in cathedrals elsewhere, including Chichester, Ripon and York. A choral society and orchestra were formed and began giving regular concerts. A wind orchestra and guitar ensemble followed. There were lunchtime staff and student recitals, professional jazz in the hall and variety concerts. In 1985 the College chamber orchestra first toured Germany, giving four concerts with great success. In 1989 Christ Church hosted the first Church Colleges Choir Festival.

The expansion of the College did not dilute its Christian ethos. This was apparent through the

Fundraising during Rag Week, 1987. (Kentish Gazette)

The start of a sponsored jailbreak for charity, 1980s. (Kentish Gazette)

many fund-raising activities which were regularly organised. Rag Week, jointly organised with UKC, raised thousands of pounds for local charities. Money came too from lunchtime concerts at the College. Holidays were arranged for disadvantaged children on the campus during the summer vacation. The College Social Action Group sponsored a child in Africa. During 1985, the year of Band Aid, a Christ Church team ran in a sponsored race to Paris against a team from Portsmouth Polytechnic.

GOVERNING

The College moved away from potential closure in the mid-1970s to a position little more than a decade later as one of the leading teacher-training institutions in the south-east with a burgeoning reputation for professional training. As Principal, Michael Berry was largely responsible for this, firstly on his own, and from 1984 onwards in partnership with his newly appointed Vice Principal, Graham Brown. As a close colleague remarked, 'Michael made that place'.

A shyer man than his predecessor, affable and principled, Michael Berry was, according to one colleague, 'a fresh breeze blowing through the place'. He would admit that communication was not one of his strengths, often keeping information close to his chest until the last moment, although he was always sympathetic to individuals who came to him with a problem. But he believed in the College, had a clear view of its future, was politically shrewd and was willing to take risks in order to achieve his vision. The governing body, chaired until his death in February 1988 by Geoffrey Templeman, and afterwards by the Bishop of Dover, was entirely supportive. Berry never believed he had all the answers and was always visiting other colleges, gleaning new ideas he might adapt in Canterbury. Looking back, he confessed that for much of the time 'one was concerned with survival, that was all that entered one's head'.

Graham Brown was a very different man in several respects. While he shared Berry's astuteness, he was a great communicator, powerfully persuasive, visible and outgoing, talented at developing contacts. One of his catchphrases was 'I'm listening to you, sunshine', which gave rise to an informal group of colleagues known as the Sunshine Club. Another of his phrases was 'I'm trying to make a shilling or two', indicative of his business-like approach.

The Berry–Brown partnership was characterised by an entrepreneurial drive which set it apart from the administration and management of most

The gardens at the back of St Martin's Priory.

Governors' meeting, 1987.

other higher education institutions of the time. Deeply committed to the College, both Principal and Vice Principal were also powerful public advocates for the College, its staff and students in difficult times. It proved to be a winning combination.

But they would also admit that the struggle would have been even harder without the cooperation and commitment of staff, teaching and non-teaching. Graham Brown had argued that, with the expansion of teacher training underpinning the development of new courses, it was critical

> *to secure the future of the College and the jobs of its staff by encouraging major changes in the pattern of the work of the College. These demand a flexibility and a readiness to adapt quickly to new conditions on the part of all concerned.*

It was a challenge which Christ Church staff more than met. There was a huge amount of goodwill towards the College from staff who were prepared to work long hours. This came partly from the Christ Church Christian ethos which had attracted sympathetic staff in the first place, who themselves had passed on the Christ Church spirit to those who came after them.

This culture could have been lost amid all the change and growth that was taking place. But Christ Church sustained a warm and friendly atmosphere, based on the belief embedded in its Anglican traditions that every individual was important. Even with more than a thousand students in the late 1980s, it was still possible for most people to know each other. While the management of the College was under the close control of the Principal and Vice Principal, structures were very flat and heads of department reported directly to Michael Berry and Graham Brown. The College was still of the size where it was possible to conduct most business informally. Keith Gwilym recalled that department heads argued their case for more money with the Vice Principal, a system known as 'Graham's back pocket'. But changes were being made to the administrative and academic management of the College, partly to rationalise roles and responsibilities, partly to match needs and resources more effectively. So several new posts were created, including Dean of Students, Dean of Studies and Director of Resources.

Budgets were constantly under pressure even while student numbers were rising so it was crucial to make the most effective use of every resource. This was why the development of new income streams, through the DHSS, NHS and NAB, was so important. It gave the College the financial flexibility critical for expansion. Tight control over resources at the centre, effectively through Berry and Brown, with the advice and assistance of successive bursars, Jim Blanthorn until 1987 and then Bill Taylor, was absolutely essential in these challenging circumstances.

Michael Berry, Principal, 1975–1997.

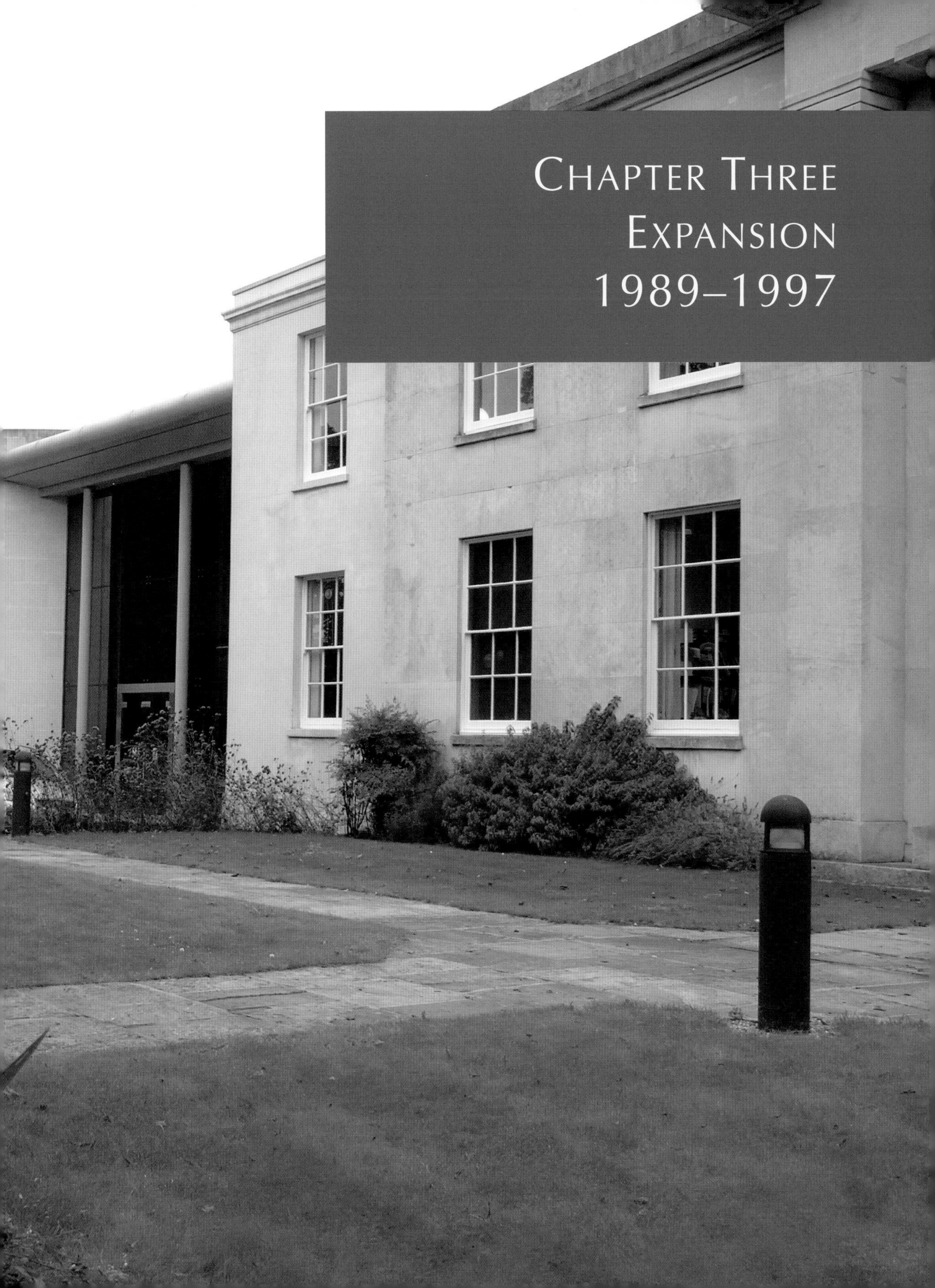

Chapter Three
Expansion
1989–1997

Public Service Education

All the hard work that secured the survival of Christ Church College during the 1980s produced during the 1990s expansion on a scale scarcely anyone except perhaps Michael Berry and Graham Brown could have foreseen. Christ Church grew from just 2,000 students at the end of the 1980s to over 6,000 by the end of 1993 and more than 10,000 by the summer of 1997. The pace of growth was remarkable but there was a clear sense of purpose on the part of the College. The mission statement prepared in 1990 declared that the College intended 'to provide higher education of quality, responsive to the intellectual and professional needs of its members and of the wider community, in a context based on Christian values'. The supporting aims emphasised not just the provision of a diverse range of professional and academic courses and qualifications. They also listed the importance of access and equal opportunities, respect for learning, the encouragement of enterprise and initiative and ethical and spiritual values. As numbers grew and pressure increased upon facilities, the governing body stressed the need to ensure that the quality of life of both staff and students was maintained. It proved to be a difficult balancing act to achieve.

Health students practising their skills.

The growth of Christ Church was driven by higher professional standards of training in healthcare. The College was well placed to take advantage of this trend. Indeed, Christ Church was often in the vanguard of such developments. The radiography programme, for instance, had been significantly enhanced in 1994 with the introduction of the clinical reporting programme for radiographers, which attracted national and international attention.

During the 1980s the College had also been involved in nursing training through curriculum development as well as tutorial work for the Canterbury and Thanet School of Nursing. At the end of the decade a major initiative to raise standards in nursing training, Project 2000, was launched. Instead of carrying out all their learning by practical experience, nurses would spend a year being taught practice and theory in a college environment. In Kent this involved the merger of the Canterbury and Thanet School with the South East Kent Schools of Nursing and Midwifery. Based on Christ Church's previous involvement, as well as the College's innovative course in occupational therapy, and thanks to the persuasive arguments of Graham Brown, the chief nursing officers of the local district health authorities agreed that the new merged School should be affiliated with the College. With the transfer of a large number of nursing staff, a new department of nursing and midwifery education was created. It was led by Peta Allen, formerly director for professional standards and development at the UK Central Council for Nursing, Midwifery and Health Visiting. The first nursing-related programme beginning in 1989 was the BSc in Nursing Studies for qualified nurses. It was the forerunner of what became a very large portfolio of post-registration studies. In September 1990 the first Project 2000 courses began with some 90 students. With the Maidstone and Medway schools of nursing soon joining the scheme, intakes rose to 150 or so every six months.

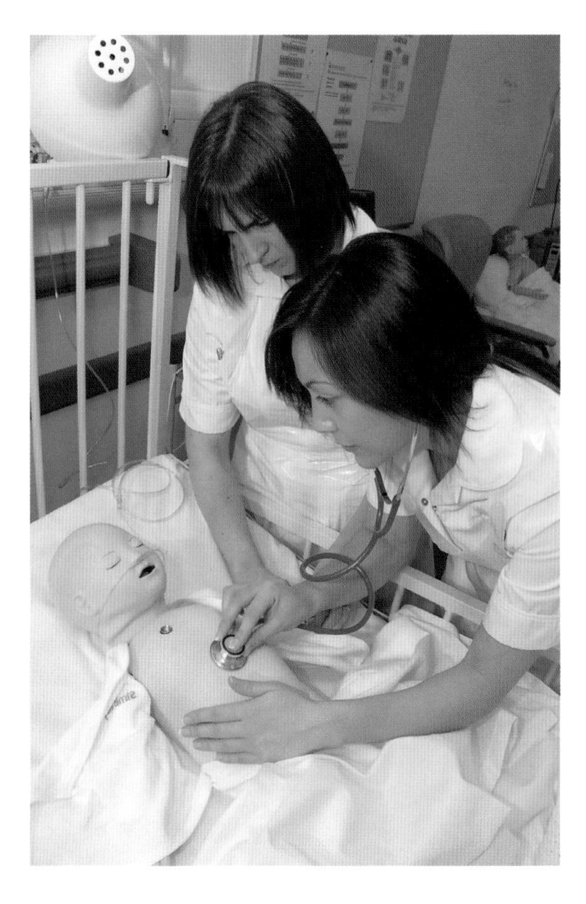

Nursing students being put through their paces by 'Sim Baby', a robotic manikin that can be programmed to display various symptoms.

At the same time the College also introduced, in partnership with the social services department of Kent County Council, a diploma in social work. In the following summer what was now the Department of Health (DH) recognised Christ Church as the Project 2000 Centre for the South-East Thames Region and a management board with representatives from both the NHS and the College was formed. Within three to four years the College was training some thousand nursing students, with established degrees in nursing studies and nursing education.

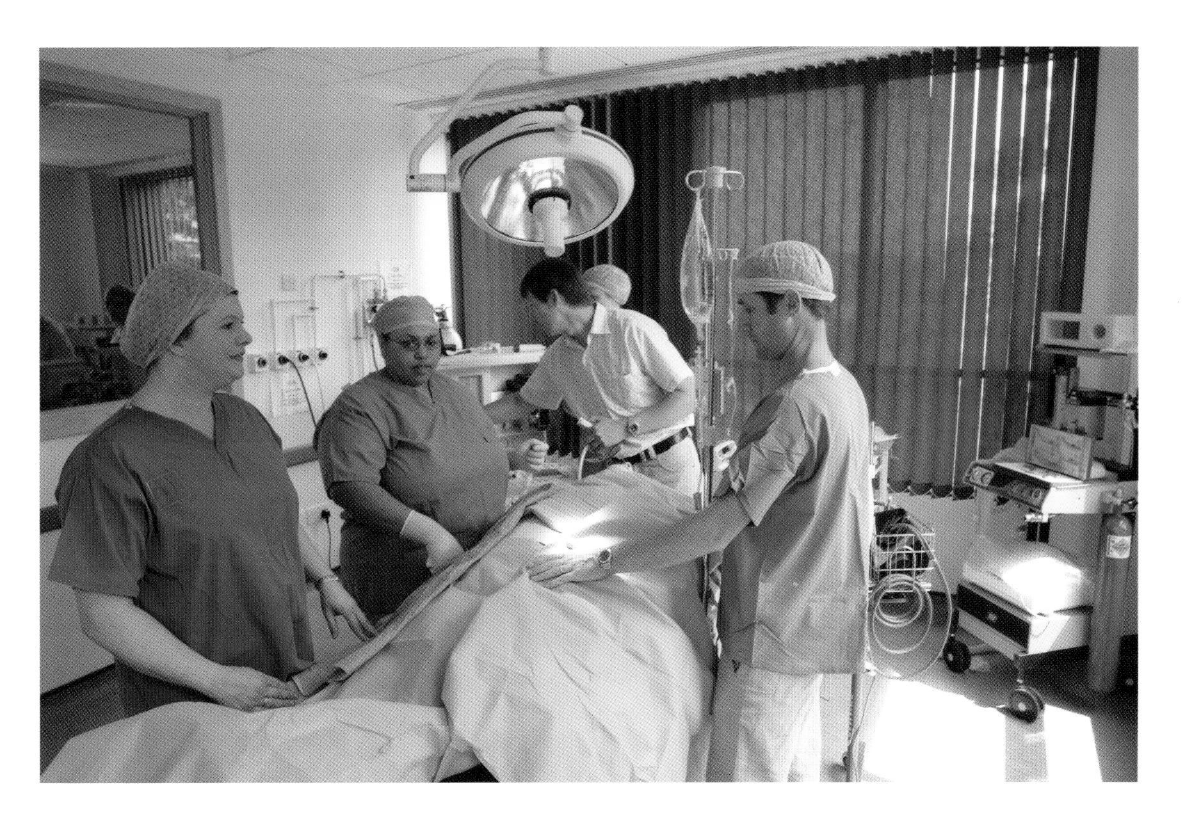

Operating Department Practice students at the Medway campus.

As well as the leadership of Peta Allan, another key to this success was the partnership approach fostered by the College. Stemming originally from the long-established relationships the College had always had with local education authorities and local schools, this had developed during the 1980s through links with major government departments and professional institutions. The success of the College's participation in Project 2000 added to its growing reputation for partnership working. The only drawback was the sense of separation from the rest of the campus although, in insisting that staff and students were accommodated alongside others following other subjects and professions, Christ Church was ahead of those who still maintained schools of nursing in their existing premises.

By the mid-1990s healthcare students accounted for a third of the College's students. But education students still remained the largest single group, making up 40 per cent of the student population. Under the direction of Margaret Alfrey, the education department continued to expand during the 1990s. This came about with the creation of the Teacher Training Agency (TTA) in 1994. The TTA carried out the most rigorous reviews and quality assessments of the training provided at all professional education colleges. As a result, there was a wave of closures, echoing those of the 1970s and 1980s. At Christ Church, Alfrey and her team, both teaching and support staff, embraced the TTA review with confidence, ensuring that all the necessary procedures were in place. When the review began, Christ Church was the twelfth largest education college. At the end of the review in 1995, Christ Church was the only primary education department awarded the highest grades, a standard it succeeded in maintaining. In 1996, for instance, an inspection by the Office for Standards in Education (Ofsted) rated primary teaching education at the College as very good. These standards were seen in the classroom. The award made by the *Times Educational Supplement* for the National Science Teacher of the Year went to Christ Church graduates twice in six years.

This was a major step forward in the evolution of education at Christ Church from teacher training to professional education faculty. Success bred success. The College was invited to take part in promoting good practice nationally and its growing reputation attracted high-calibre external examiners. The College was the first in England to be invited to join the Internationalisation of Teacher Education, through exchanges and joint study programmes with similar institutions in Scandinavia, other parts of Europe and America. Research work expanded, staff were encouraged to take PhDs and a taught doctorate was introduced. By the late 1990s the College was the third largest provider of professional education in the country with an outstanding reputation in professional primary education.

An important influence upon the success of the department was the advantage it made of its location as well as its proximity to London. Kent, with its diverse economic nature, from prosperity to deprivation, and inner-city London provided a wide range of experience for education students. Through the Urban Learning Foundation, the College was linked with several other voluntary colleges with a base in east London, where Christ Church was also involved from 1992 onwards with the YMCA George Williams College

Teacher-training students performing a science experiment.

Head of Postgraduate Initial Teacher Education, Dr John Moss, middle, teaching drama to secondary teacher trainees.

in Walthamstow. Through George Williams, Christ Church offered degree and diploma courses in youth work and informal education.

Another spin-off within the education department came through the introduction of the Certificate of Education (Post-Compulsory) for teachers in further and higher education colleges and police colleges. As a result, the College became more involved with staff development in colleges and expanded its work with police colleges. Here was another avenue opening up in the College's developing portfolio of professional public service education.

The College's success in healthcare and professional education produced further benefits since the example of many of those returning to the workplace with enhanced degrees encouraged their colleagues to do the same thing. Another consequence from the strides made by the education department was to compel other departments to become more independent. As the nature of teacher training altered, it was no longer possible for trainee teachers to spend time studying other subjects alongside other students. So, from 1996, as education students took all their courses within the education department, other departments had to begin recruiting more students to make up the difference.

The creation of the specialist educationist was matched by the creation of the specialist academic. In 1989, when Dr Terence Clifford-Amos joined the English department, of which he later became head, it offered only a single programme of joint honours plus a PGCE. He was teaching trainee teachers, international relations and English, with some research squeezed in.

Within a decade all this had changed. More programmes were devised, the first single honours degrees were introduced and research

The main areas of interest of the Ecology Research Group are applied and predator ecology and molluscan biology.

became a priority. Single honours degrees became available in a wide variety of subjects, from music to applied social sciences and sports science. Teaching standards at degree level were steadily improving in parallel with higher admission standards. The proof was in the examination results. Between 1984 and 1990 the percentage of upper second degrees awarded rose from 14 per cent to 46 per cent. Staff appraisal was introduced in 1993. Conferences, short courses, exchanges, publishing, editing, study leave and the pursuit of higher qualifications were all ways staff were encouraged to develop their skills. An inspection in 1992 rated history and religious studies as very good and geography as good. In the same year the College achieved the second highest rating among all general colleges in the first Research Assessment Exercise (RAE), outstripping several of the former polytechnics which had gained university status. In the following year history gained a quality assessment of excellent from the Higher Education Funding Council for England (HEFCE), the first such rating awarded to a non-university. This owed much to the leadership of the head of department, Sean Greenwood. In 1995 geography, developed under the direction of Richard Goodenough, gained a similar rating. In 1996, when Sean Greenwood became the first person from within the College to hold the title of professor, the RAE graded four subjects – education, history, theology and music – as 3a, that is, work with the

The Research Assessment Exercise (RAE) commended the Ecology Research Group's work on birds of prey.

potential to reach levels of national importance. The RAE rated research at Christ Church, such as the work of the Ecology Research Centre on molluscs, birds of prey and biological control of pests more highly than at any other general college of higher education.

The development of academic research covered students as well as staff. In 1990, when Gordon Diaper became the first Christ Church student to gain a PhD, there were 17 students studying for the MPhil or PhD and 142 studying for the MA. Four years later Maurice Vile moved from UKC to become director of research at the College and a postgraduate centre was established. International relationships were established across the curriculum with bodies such as University College, Cork, Faro Polytechnic in Portugal, University College, Kristianstad, in Sweden and the University of Thessaloniki in Greece.

The realisation that the College could compete with the newest universities made Michael Berry and his colleagues wonder why the College should not achieve similar status. Such an aspiration was almost unheard of but then Berry was a man who often thought the unthinkable. University status would also help with the promotion of the College overseas. This was a significant part of College activities by the early 1990s, particularly for the additional funding it brought in. The College was also undertaking overseas consultancy work, for instance in South Africa, Malaysia and Eastern Europe. But the College found itself at a disadvantage because the word 'university' did not appear in its title. The College decided to apply for the title of University College, held by so many of the College's overseas partners, but the government turned down the idea on principle in 1993. Instead the College followed an alternative route and decided to seek the power to award its own degrees and other qualifications, initially in respect of taught programmes but with the intention of doing so for supervised research programmes as well. It was to the College's advantage that in 1992 UKC, the validating authority, had awarded Christ Church accredited institution status, giving the College responsibility for the design, examination and standards of all taught courses. So at the end of 1995 Christ Church became entitled to award its own degrees. With this achievement to its credit, the College once again applied to be known as Canterbury Christ Church University College. With pressure building up from other similar institutions to change their names, the trend was in Christ Church's favour. But it would take another three years and a change in legislation before there was any result.

ENVIRONMENT

If the Canterbury campus struggled during the 1980s to meet the needs of the College, during the 1990s it was almost overwhelmed by the pace of growth. Expansion was driven by numbers, for with numbers came money. So there was always a time lag between more students arriving and the appointment of more staff and the completion of new buildings and facilities, in that order. Terence Clifford-Amos remembered that 'the place was jam-packed – it was almost impossible to get a coffee'. But there was never any sense that the College was struggling to develop the resources it needed. There was vibrancy about the place which came with growth. The accelerating progress of the College was palpable.

There was still space to be developed on campus. David Coupe's master-plan from the 1980s still held good. But such space had to be carefully utilised if the attractive atmosphere of the campus was to remain intact. Ultimately this meant that just as student accommodation had been acquired off campus, so would buildings for other uses. In the meantime, the £2.5 million paramedical centre was opened in 1989, funded largely through the NHS. This was followed by the refurbishment of the refectory, the improvement of IT facilities and the addition of several extensions to the library. Since the growth of the College seemed incessant, so too did developments on campus, and at times it seemed to have become a permanent building site.

Off campus more student accommodation was leased, mainly at Pin Hill in Canterbury. Study bedrooms were created in a block, later named Lanfranc, in Northgate, the first time the College had borrowed money to fund a development. In 1992 the College acquired a

The original entrance to the Sessions House.

Working in the art studio.

Salomons House was bought by Sir David Salomons in 1829 and stayed in family hands for three generations.

property in St Peter's Lane. Renamed the Marlowe Centre, it housed the art and design department. A former hospital, The Mount, in Stodmarsh Road, purchased in the same year, became the postgraduate centre. (Both these properties would be sold in later years to fund even greater growth.) A property on Lady Wootton's Green was acquired in 1993 to house language studies. In 1994 another Northgate block was leased to provide more office accommodation.

One of the most significant acquisitions was the Old Sessions House next door to the North Holmes Road campus. An important historic building in its own right, for many years the principal courthouse in the city, once linked directly to the cells of the neighbouring prison, it had been built in 1810 and incongruously

extended in the 1970s. The College bought the building in 1995 and embarked upon a major three-year redevelopment project which David Coupe would handle with the aesthetic appreciation and sensitivity appropriate for such a building. The cost of this scheme was met from the surplus funds the College had been accumulating from varying sources of revenue. HEFCE's unit funding policy also benefited Christ Church, with its small but carefully managed campus and lots of students.

The College became owners of an even grander building in 1995. This was Salomons, hidden in the heart of Kent, west of Canterbury, close by Tunbridge Wells. Taking its name after the eminent family who developed the house and estate during the 19th century, Salomons was a sprawling late-Victorian mansion delightfully situated

in 38 acres. Formerly known as Broomhill, it had been the country residence of Sir David Salomons, the first Jew to become Lord Mayor of London. It took its current form, including what was the largest private theatre in the country, under his nephew, also David. An inventive amateur scientist, he also organised the first motor show in England, he was a talented photographer who experimented with film, he devised an automatic railway signalling system and his home was the first house in England to use electricity for purposes other than lighting. The house eventually passed into public ownership and by the 1990s was run by South Thames Regional Health Authority as an accredited institute offering courses in health and social care, including a taught doctorate in clinical psychology. It housed centres for applied social and psychological development and for leadership and management development and had established a profitable business as a conference venue. Why would Christ Church be

Top left: Sir David Salomons, 1797–1873.
Top right: The accumulator room for storing electricity. Salomons was one of the first houses in Britain to have electricity.
Bottom left: Sir David Lionel Salomons, 1851–1925, a keen scientist, engineer and pioneer of motor transport. He organised the world's first motor show in 1895 and, above right, built a 'Science Theatre' to demostrate experiments.
Botttom right: The theatre houses the famous Welte organ and is used for special events.

interested in such a property so far from Canterbury? That was partly the reason – to establish a base in the west of Kent. There were two other obvious attractions – the healthcare and social work courses, particularly the doctorate in clinical psychology, broadened the College's involvement in this sector; while the conference business was yet another independent income stream. The property was also relatively inexpensive. There was a lot of competition but the College rarely let an opportunity slip past. It was the last major deal concluded under the Berry–Brown regime and epitomised their positive, forward-thinking and entrepreneurial approach to the development of the College.

An even more ambitious plan was being examined at the same time. In 1994 the governing body first considered whether or not the College should develop a completely new campus on the outskirts of the city. Two years later, the College had identified a possible site on the New Dover Road leading out of the city but plans had only reached the stage of negotiating with the site's owners. If the College wished to take the proposal any further, there was still much work to do, not least in persuading the City Council that it had any advantages.

Salomons is set in 36 acres of magnificent gardens and parkland.

LIVING

The dramatic six-fold rise in the number of College students, most of whom were living off campus, inevitably made an impact on Canterbury. After a number of incidents, an initiative was started in the early 1990s to ease tension and improve relations through Dr Terence Clifford-Amos from the College with the help of the city's MP, Julian Brazier, and the Lord Mayor, Clive Wake. This was known as the Town and Gown Forum, which brought together representatives from the city's higher education institutions, including their student bodies, the city council, the police and other interested parties. This helped to draw up guidelines for student life within Canterbury and succeeded in improving relationships as well as behaviour.

The College, in formulating its own disciplinary procedures and providing advice to students, was always very aware of its neighbourly responsibilities. But the links between Christ Church and the wider community were relatively limited. The relationship with the city council, where some members regarded the student population as a social burden rather than an economic and cultural benefit, was not always easy. Public relations, rather than the development of functional partnerships, was not one of the Principal's strong points and in any case, in the days of centralised management, he had plenty of other issues to deal with.

There were ways in which the College sought to reach out to those beyond the campus limits. Links with business came through the Business Development Unit (which later became the Centre for Enterprise and Business Development) created in 1992, and in the

Concert in Canterbury Cathedral.

Above left: Carols by candlelight in Canterbury Cathedral.

Above right: Master of the Queen's music, Sir Peter Maxwell Davies is a regular visitor to the University. He is shown here rehearsing his Naxos Quartet no 8 *which was was premiered by the Maggini Quartet at St Gregory's Centre for Music in 2006.*

Small Business Forum, which aimed to generate business involvement in College courses. One of the most visible ways in which the College connected with the outside world was through music. Under Grenville Hancox, this became one of the most outstanding aspects of the College. Hancox believed that music should be more than part of academic studies. It had to be a challenging and life-changing experience of benefit to the wider community. From the late 1980s the College developed unparalleled opportunities for staff and students to take part in making music. From an early stage the College made a significant contribution towards the annual music festival in the city. The College art centre at St Gregory's was the regular venue for weekly lunchtime concerts open to the public. In 1991, for the enthronement of Dr George Carey as the new archbishop, Hancox arranged and conducted music for a special programme broadcast by the BBC. Links with eminent contemporary composers elevated Christ Church's musical reputation. Most notably, the Maggini Quartet became the College's quartet in residence in 1993. Music became a well-established and welcome ambassador for the College while, in being a central part of College life, it restored a musical link to an ancient site, connecting the College with a distant monastic past, sharing a Christian, academic and musical heritage.

The College's musical achievements showed that a vibrant life could be achieved despite cramped and inadequate facilities. Not only were teaching and learning facilities as well as student accommodation over-stretched, so too were the College's sports facilities. Inadequate sports provision was a major consideration, along with the crowded city-centre site, behind the plans for a new campus. Pressure of space claimed existing facilities, such as the campus squash courts, which disappeared in 1995, replaced by another learning centre. Those not requisitioned for other purposes were creaking under the strain of supporting many more students than ever envisaged. In 1992, for instance, the Stodmarsh Road playing fields had to be closed for reasons of health and safety. Reopened three years later, with enhanced changing rooms, they still provided only one rugby and two soccer pitches, when the College already fielded three teams in each sport, over uneven ground which had a tendency to become waterlogged. With other higher priorities, the only new sporting development was an indoor fitness centre and even that was established only after considerable difficulty. But in spite of these problems, the College, both through individuals and teams, still made an impact on the world of sport. In 1995, for instance, one student, Simon Wiseman, represented Great Britain in the World Triathlon Championships in New Zealand; another, Nikki Milne, played for the Ireland women's rugby team; and the men's tennis team reached the British Universities Sports Association (BUSA) national final.

The expansion of the College also brought a change in the composition of the student body. While most students taking teaching and nursing courses remained predominantly female, an increasing number of College students were mature and part-time. Even in 1990 a quarter of the annual intake was over the age of 23; while almost half of all students in 1995 were part-time. This change, combined with increasing financial pressures on students, significantly increased the caseload for the Students' Union welfare officer. In 1995 she wrote in her annual report that she had been overwhelmed by students coming to see her with problems over money, work and personal relationships. A student counsellor was also appointed who dealt with marital breakdowns, violence within relationships, drug, alcohol and gambling addictions, and sexual and racial harassment. There was also a need to consider the very different requirements of mature students.

Rugby – Canterbury Christ Church University has two squads in the BUSA league.

Next page: The Annual Carol Service in Canterbury Cathedral.

Governing

With many more students doing many more courses funded by bodies other than the education department, Christ Church became more financially secure. By the early 1990s, more than half of all the College's income came from bodies other than HEFCE. Money from the Church was never requested but money was rarely borrowed either. The assets on the North Holmes Road campus still belonged to the Church so the College itself had no security for any borrowing. The Lanfranc development, off campus, was the first instance of the College taking out a loan. The College's income rose steadily, exceeding £30 million by the mid-1990s.

For most of this period the management of the College remained effectively in the hands of Michael Berry and his deputy, Graham Brown. Academic matters, however, were largely dealt with through committees comprising heads of department where decisions were reached through consensus. While this system helped to prevent the isolation of departments from each other, it was becoming cumbersome. By the end of the 1990s there were 18 heads of department and the idea of creating faculties was being discussed. For staff, as the College grew, the focus shifted from the common room to the departments and the intimate social life embracing all staff possible in a smaller institution inevitably began to disappear. For students, relationships with the College authorities were settled, amicable and cooperative, increasing student participation on College committees doing much to improve communications. The governing

body was helped in its relations with all parts of the College during such a momentous period in its history by the calibre of its chairmen. The Bishop of Dover was succeeded in 1992 by Dr Bill Petty, Kent's director of education, who handed over to Brigadier Maurice Atherton in 1994. Brigadier Atherton, with his brisk, incisive and business-like approach in chairing the governing body and several of its committees, played an important role in driving forward the development of the College.

One thing the College had always lacked was a proper coat of arms, using an unofficial version for many years. During 1991 the College librarian, Tony Edwards, who would retire in the following year, assisted the Norroy and Ulster King of Arms in drawing up arms and a motto for the College. The grant of arms was finally awarded to the College by the Garter King of Arms on All Saints' Day, 1 November 1991. Using the College colours, in heraldic terms bleu celeste and sanguine, the arms used four crosses to denote the College's Church foundation. Links with Canterbury were represented through a Cornish chough taken from the arms of St Thomas Becket, and by the lion in the College crest which came from the City of Canterbury. The motto, *'veritas liberabit vos'* or 'the truth shall make you free', was taken from St John's Gospel. A formal presentation was made at Congregation on 30 November.

The official coat of arms, 1991. The four crosses denote the College's Church foundation. The black bird is taken from the arms of St Thomas Becket who was murdered in Canterbury Cathedral in 1170 and the Latin motto translates as 'Truth shall make you free'.

In March 1996 Michael Berry gave notice to the governors that he wished to retire at the end of the 1996/97 academic year. There was no slowdown in the development of the College during his final year as Principal. In October 1996 Professor Tricia David gave the inaugural lecture marking the founding of the Centre for International Studies in Early Childhood. In December the first Christ Church students occupied Lanfranc and work began on yet another building on the North Holmes Road campus. In spring 1997 Christ Church was among only six out of 66 primary teacher-training institutions to achieve four grade-one assessments through Ofsted. Plans were made for improvements to the Old Sessions House, including a new extension with lecture theatre. During Michael Berry's last term the final preparations were being made to introduce a BSc honours degree in policing with Kent Constabulary. Three students distinguished themselves in the sporting arena – Nikki Harvey won the UK tenpin bowling championship for the second year running and Lynsey Tee the UK trampolining championship for the third time in a row, while an international student, Aragon St Charles, won a third international lacrosse cap for Germany. With numbers of students now approaching 10,000, Michael Berry was leaving an impressive base on which his successor might build.

Top right: Kent Police's Assistant Chief Constable Allyn Thomas (left) and Dr Keith Gwilym Pro-Vice Chancellor (Dean of Business and Sciences). A new fleet of police cars carrying the University's logo recognise the relationship between the University and the Police Service.

Bottom right: The University's police community support officer at the Canterbury campus.

POLICE
POLICE
Canterbury
Christ Church
University
Training Kent's Police Officers
Kent
Police

KENT
POLICE

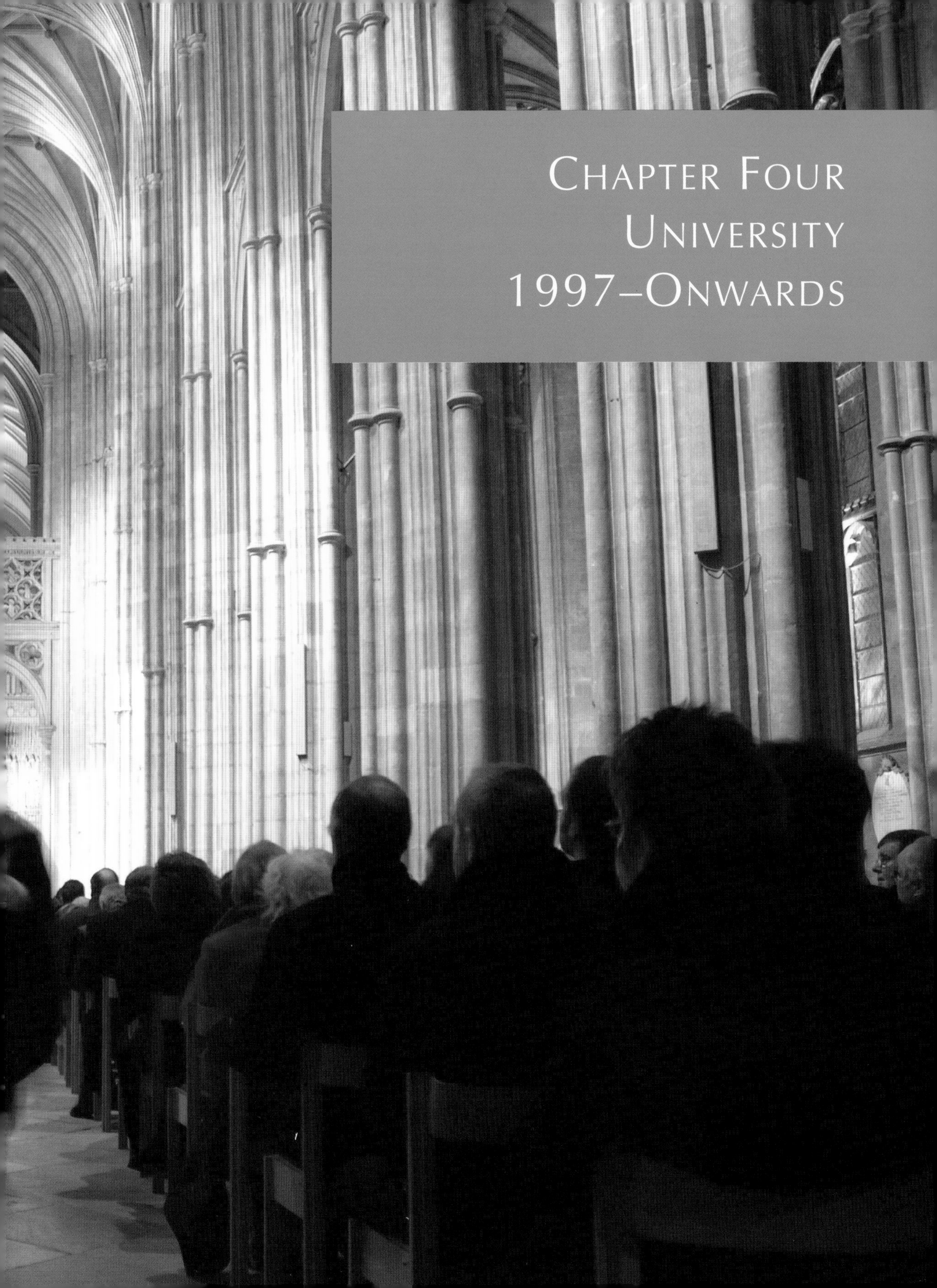

Chapter Four
University
1997–Onwards

Looking Outwards

The new Principal, Michael Wright, took the helm on 1 September 1997. Aged 48 at the time of his appointment, he had graduated in law at Birmingham University. Specialising in employment law, he lectured in law at Bristol Polytechnic before moving to Glasgow College of Technology where he was head of department from 1980 until 1983. Moving to Napier College in 1983 as Dean of Business Studies, he was appointed successively Assistant Principal and Vice Principal. Closely involved with Napier's successful application in 1992 for university status, he was Deputy Vice Chancellor at the time of his departure for Canterbury. He seemed an ideal appointment for Christ Church, especially given the part he had also played at Napier in developing the campus and bringing nursing into the university. He also appreciated from working with Napier's first Vice Chancellor, Professor William Turmeau, the benefit Napier derived from promoting itself to the wider community.

For Christ Church, this latter task was inextricably bound up with achieving university status. Wright was convinced that the College would need to continue to grow if it was to justify university status in a city which already contained a well-established university. Christ Church, a servant of the community ever since it had first opened its doors, sending out young men and women into local schools and then into local hospitals, had never shouted about the value of the work it did. Now was the time to raise the College's profile.

Michael Wright, Principal since 1997 and now Vice Chancellor, with students.

A student at Broadstairs campus.

This was particularly important not just in the College's quest for university status. Michael Wright came to Canterbury only a few months after the election of the new Labour government which had famously proclaimed 'education, education, education' as its first priority, with health running it a close second. The further opportunity for the growth of the College was there to be seized. But the increasing size of the College would once again mean overcoming the challenges of the past writ large – the pressures of more students on accommodation and facilities, the need for more staff, the imperative to ensure that students and residents lived harmoniously side by side, the importance of careful financial planning, and the priority of sustaining the welcoming, friendly nature of a Church college.

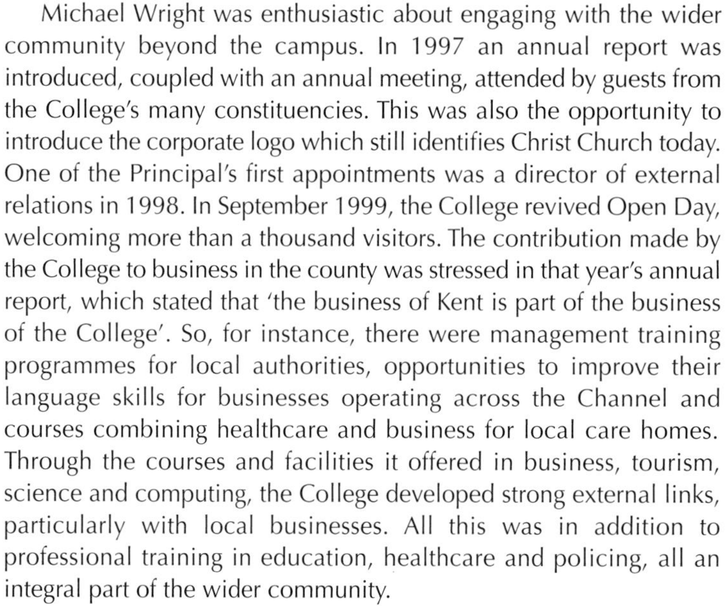

Michael Wright was enthusiastic about engaging with the wider community beyond the campus. In 1997 an annual report was introduced, coupled with an annual meeting, attended by guests from the College's many constituencies. This was also the opportunity to introduce the corporate logo which still identifies Christ Church today. One of the Principal's first appointments was a director of external relations in 1998. In September 1999, the College revived Open Day, welcoming more than a thousand visitors. The contribution made by the College to business in the county was stressed in that year's annual report, which stated that 'the business of Kent is part of the business of the College'. So, for instance, there were management training programmes for local authorities, opportunities to improve their language skills for businesses operating across the Channel and courses combining healthcare and business for local care homes. Through the courses and facilities it offered in business, tourism, science and computing, the College developed strong external links, particularly with local businesses. All this was in addition to professional training in education, healthcare and policing, all an integral part of the wider community.

Michael Wright and his team believed that the College still had much to offer its host community. The new Principal himself would lead by example, with his involvement in the health authority, Thanet College, the Duke of York's Royal Military School and Canterbury Cathedral. The College's annual report for 2002 described the College's daily work as 'a crucial part of the social, economic and cultural infrastructure of Kent'. With most students in one of the largest non-metropolitan areas in England and Wales still looking beyond its boundaries for their higher education, an expanding College offered them greater incentives to remain. The College, in emphasising teaching-led academic work and professional education, was

Broadstairs campus.

complementary to, rather than competing with, UKC. But the College also wanted to reach out to those parts of Kent and the Medway where it had been a struggle to offer opportunities in higher education to young people.

The College had a history of taking part in joint educational initiatives, most notably through the Urban Learning Foundation. With this background, and with the political tide swelling in favour of wider access to higher education, the College embarked upon an ambitious programme in 1999. Chris Bounds – who had been at the College since 1977, was appointed Dean of Studies in 1988 and would become Vice-Principal in 2002 – pointed out to Michael Wright a gaping hole in the College's catchment area. On the Isle of Thanet, centred around Broadstairs, with a population of 130,000, there was a thriving college of further education but scarcely any opportunities for higher education. It was an economically deprived area, with high unemployment and low incomes, where 94 per cent of young people did not move on to higher education. With Christ Church already acting as the validating authority for Thanet College, the time seemed ripe for trying to plug the gap. Thanet College supported the idea, as did Thanet District Council, which provided land, and HEFCE, which allocated student numbers and funding to the new venture. It was

speedily achieved. In January 2000 the first sod was cut on site and in September the first students took up residence. The official opening was performed by the Archbishop of Canterbury on 1 December. One of the key individuals in making it all happen was Roger Clayton, the College's Assistant Principal (Business), who had been appointed in 1995 to oversee the management of resources. A second phase of further development was completed in 2001. This was the Allen Building, named after a local Second World War fighter pilot and winner of the Distinguished Flying Cross, containing social facilities, resources for the study of popular music, technology and digital media, plus a health skills laboratory. Residential accommodation (Northwood Halls) came next in 2003, the same year in which the College marked its 40th anniversary with a visit to the Broadstairs campus by the Duke of York. By the following year, approximately a thousand students were pursuing courses at Broadstairs.

In that year, 2004, a new Archbishop of Canterbury had performed another opening ceremony on behalf of the College. This time the site was further north, at Chatham, on the Medway, where Christ Church became a partner on a new campus, developed from the former Royal Naval School, where the University of Greenwich (UG) was already established. This time Christ Church's participation stemmed mainly from the College's entrepreneurial spirit, which still flourished under Michael Wright, offering the College's existing skills in courses not provided by other partners to a wider

The £8 million, Grade II-listed Drill Hall Library is thought to be the longest open library space in Europe. It is part of the Universities at Medway development, shared by students from Canterbury Christ Church, Kent and Greenwich.

Top left and right: Medway campus facility is located in a new, custom-designed building on the Chatham Maritime site, close to the historic Chatham Dockyard. Canterbury Christ Church at Medway specializes in health, education and police programmes.

Bottom right: Many of Medway's students are mature and courses are designed to be flexible.

audience. Rowan Williams Court, as the Christ Church building was named, included a full health skills laboratory, with two hospital wards, a paediatric and midwifery suite, operating theatre and suites for radiography and occupational therapy. When the Archbishop visited Chatham in October 2004, the first 40 police students from Kent Constabulary had also started their training course in the building. The Universities at Medway project, as it became known, was funded jointly by the three partners, including not only UG and Christ Church but also UKC. One of the most remarkable developments was the shared learning resource centre transformed from the former drill hall. Opened in February 2006, this was funded by all the partners. Although the partnership restricted future expansion, Christ Church was educating more than a thousand students at Chatham within a year, many of them being mature students living locally.

Having demonstrated the regenerating power of education with such success at Broadstairs, the College looked outwards once more towards an equally disadvantaged part of the county. This time the focus of attention was Folkestone, a once-prosperous seaside resort and port fallen, like Broadstairs, on hard times, a casualty of changing social tastes. Discussions about the College's involvement began shortly after the inauguration of the first Arts, Well-Being and Health programme at Christ Church in 2002 which, as the title suggested, aimed to foster health and well-being through involvement in the arts. The healing attributes of music, for instance, were vigorously promoted within the College's music department where Grenville Hancox and Stephen Clift were carrying out research into the ability of music to provide relief for sufferers of dementia. This eventually led, among other developments, to the formation of the non-profit organisation, Sing For Your Life, which offered musical opportunities for older people in care and people with dementia. One of the catalysts for the College's links with Folkestone was Roger De Haan, whose father had founded Saga, the travel operator for older people. He himself had played a key role in the further success of the business but he also had a deep interest in Folkestone, his home area. He was also interested in research into relief for dementia which his father had suffered from during his latter years. The College and Roger De Haan came together to develop a centre in Folkestone to investigate the links between the arts and good health, not just for older people but also for families and young children. Opened in Folkestone's Creative Quarter in the Old Town in 2004, the Sidney De Haan Research Centre for Arts and Health was named after the founder of Saga and funded by the Roger De Haan Charitable Trust, which also funded the South-East Dementia Centre based at the Christ Church campus in Canterbury.

At the same time the Creative Foundation, in which the principal educational partners were Christ Church and the University of Greenwich, was spearheading the development of higher education in and around Folkestone. Sue Piotrowski in particular was a driving force in this initiative which saw the launch of a foundation degree programme featuring a new course in the performing arts. Christ Church participated in another collaborative venture. This was the Folkestone People's History Centre, which also

Above: The Glassworks is part of Folkestone's new Creative Quarter.

Below: University Centre Folkestone welcomed its first students in 2007. Subjects offered include performing and visual arts, business and enterprise.

Through the Hall Place Enterprise Centre, Kent businesses can access a wide variety of business support and training opportunities.

opened in the Old Town, and intended to develop with the involvement of local people an internet archive of the town's history.

More widely, the College, through its Centre for Enterprise and Business Development, which eventually relocated to Hall Place on the outskirts of Canterbury, delivered training, services and events to foster the growth of business in the region. The international dimension of the College's activities was already well developed in the late 1990s. In 1997, 260 full-time equivalent overseas students drawn from 30 countries were studying at Christ Church. The College was already involved with the Erasmus programme, through which students from other European nations had the chance to study in the UK. There were also exchange links with North Carolina and North Illinois State Universities. Stronger relationships were being forged with partners just over the Channel. In March 1998 a partnership agreement for joint projects in language teaching was signed in Boulogne with the Université de Littoral. Three years later, the College's media department was working on animation with ESAAT (École Supérieur des Arts Appliqués et du Textile) based at Roubaix near Lille. In 2003, building on earlier connections, a staff and student exchange agreement was signed with the Université Catholique de Lille, an institution similar to Christ Church, whose secular nature was underpinned by a church mission. This led, three years later, after thorough validation, to the first double degree course in English in the UK, leading to a BA in English at Canterbury and the Licence des Lettres at Lille.

The Path To University

The political impetus for wider access to higher education, an aim seized by the College through the development of the campuses at Broadstairs and Chatham as well as continued growth at Canterbury, led to a further remarkable rise in the numbers of students coming to Christ Church. These rose from 10,000 in 1997 to more than 14,000 five years later. At the turn of the millennium three-quarters of these came from Kent, three-quarters were female, half were part-time and almost two-thirds were over the age of 21. From a diverse range of backgrounds, they were spread almost equally between professional education, healthcare and other subjects. Christ Church had become one of the largest non-university institutions of higher education in England.

Michael Wright and students celebrating Canterbury Christ Church's full university title, 2005.

Canterbury
Christ Church
University

Above: The Archbishop of Canterbury was installed as the University's first Chancellor at the inauguration service in the cathedral on 12 December 2005.

Right: The inauguration service celebrated full university status. From left to right: Peter Hermitage (Deputy Pro-Chancellor), Bishop Stephen Venner (Pro-Chancellor), Archbishop Rowan Williams (Chancellor), Professor Michael Wright (Vice Chancellor), Professor Christopher Bounds (Deputy Vice Chancellor) and Alan Connolly (Mace Bearer).

Such expansion brought its own challenges but did nothing to impede the improving quality of the education offered at Christ Church. Throughout this period inspections by Ofsted of the primary and secondary education programmes were consistently good, while programmes not funded by the Teacher Training Agency received very positive reports from the Quality Assurance Agency (QAA) for Higher Education. Courses in health and social care, expanding steadily, were also monitored regularly by the relevant professional authorities. (The Teacher Training Agency has now been replaced by the Training and Development Agency.)

Prior to Michael Berry's retirement in 1997 the governing body had already approved a change of name to Canterbury Christ Church University College, winning the support of the Archbishop of Canterbury as Visitor. But objections from other quarters were raised and it was decided to wait until the law was changed. Christ Church was finally able to adopt its new name in 1998 under the Teaching and Higher Education Act. Under Michael Wright, the College delayed its application for the power to award research degrees, which had to be accompanied by an application for the title of 'university'. (Research students based at Christ Church received degrees awarded by the University of Kent.) It was in any case likely that the criteria for acceptance would be changed, and the intervening period gave the College time to expand in new directions as well as within the Canterbury campus. The criteria for university status were finally revised in 2003 by which time Christ Church had developed rapidly. The time had come for the College to submit its request for university status. This was certainly impressive. The College could demonstrate a winning combination of a well-established Christian foundation, a past record of achievement and, based on its present activities, a future full of potential through its contribution to the region, its overseas links and a character complementary to UKC.

The good news was received in Canterbury in the summer of 2005. Privy Council consent entitled the College to be known as Canterbury Christ Church University. In acknowledging that Christ Church had in effect been functioning as a university in all but name, it was also a testament to the commitment and belief of generations of staff and the leadership of each Principal. It was in particular a tribute to the hard work of Chris Bounds in the pursuit of consistent standards of academic achievement. The announcement immediately raised the profile of the College. The new University celebrated the achievement on 22 September, followed on 12 December by the inauguration of the University with the installation of the Archbishop of Canterbury in the cathedral as the first Chancellor. From the city council came the gift of a university mace. Christ Church had come of age.

ENVIRONMENT

The opportunity for Christ Church to build a presence in Broadstairs and Chatham came in part from the failure of the plans to develop a completely new campus on the outskirts of Canterbury. Approval of the idea, which ground to a halt on local and environmental objections, would have absorbed the money Christ Church was able to put to good use elsewhere in Kent.

Although plans for the new Canterbury campus were abandoned, there was an ever-increasing need to find more space, more student residences, more sports facilities, better arts and music provision and better facilities for health, education and business training. Christ Church remained committed to doing as much as possible to improve facilities in Canterbury.

Above: Netball.

Right: Students walking past the Powell Building which is named after Michael Powell, the disinguished film director.

Invicta &

Top left: Michael Powell, left, and Emeric Pressburger, right, wrote, directed and produced some of the most memorable and inventive British films of the 20th century.

Top right: Posters for The Life and Death of Colonel Blimp *and* The Red Shoes, *1940s.*

Bottom left: Dan Richards, right, Canterbury Christ Church's first animator in residence, discussing his film, Windmill Boy, *which was premiered in the Powell Building, 2006.*

The skill of Christ Church's architect, David Coupe, lay in incorporating yet more new buildings within a constricted site while maintaining its special ambience. In March 1998 the media department was relocated in another new purpose-built block. This was later named the Powell Building after Michael Powell, the distinguished British film director, a native of Kent, and housed a research centre dedicated to the films of Powell and Pressburger. At the same time, existing buildings were refurbished, particularly the students' union, the refectory and St Martin's Priory. Just off the site, the refurbished and extended Old Sessions House was opened in November 1998, providing a most impressive and spacious complex for professional education.

Runcie Court, named after Archbishop Runcie, was originally the grand stables block built by Sir David Salomons in the 1890s. The design was inspired by a French chateau and the stables accommodated 21 horses and a coach house for 12 large carriages. Today's conversion has been careful to maintain the original features of the building. The site has a specialist library, a purpose built interview training suite, IT facilities and a café.

In the same year the west wing of the former stable block at Salomons was converted into offices and other ancillary accommodation. The opportunities offered at Salomons were also extended when from the beginning of 2000 the College of Guidance Studies, which trained careers officers, was transferred from Hextable to form the Centre for Career and Personal Development within the Department of Post-Compulsory Education. Through this partnership, which revived student numbers, a valuable resource was saved which might otherwise have been lost.

With the limitations of the Canterbury site, Christ Church has continued to look around the city for suitable properties. In 2001 the College bought 21 New Dover Road, and turned it into offices and seminar rooms. A former garage site was purchased in 2002 and developed as student accommodation, opening in 2003. At the same time, the first phase of development of the Student Village began on a brownfield site in Parham Road. Also in 2003, Hall Place, an imposing mansion at Harbledown on the edge of the city, was taken over. After being extensively refurbished, it housed the Centre for Enterprise and Business Development, Department for Professional Development and the Centre for Education Leadership and Schools Improvement. In August 2004 Christ Church seized the opportunity to make another important property acquisition. Clarkson House, a modern office block on the Canterbury ring road, has been renamed Augustine House and will provide a much-needed new library, learning resource and student ancillary services centre.

Learning

With facilities and accommodation dispersed so widely, not only within Canterbury but across several different sites, the challenge has been to make them work effectively. While the distance between buildings in Canterbury is probably less than on the campuses of other large and long-established universities, there are few higher education institutions operating several campuses as far apart as those at Canterbury, Salomons, Broadstairs and Medway. Ever since the Broadstairs project was first considered, Michael Wright has been determined to ensure that all Christ Church students, wherever they are based, should share the same standard of experience. Ultimately this depends on continuing investment in improved facilities throughout the University but it has also relied on the capable leadership of those in charge of the various sites and the willingness of staff to move between locations. This can be a trying task on today's crowded roads, but given the commendations of successive inspection reports, it has obviously proved worthwhile, allowing the University to offer any student, on any course and at any location the same standard of teaching.

Graduation – Canterbury Christ Church University is the largest centre of higher education in Kent for the major public services – teacher training, policing and health and social care.

Above and opposite: Graduation day.

The rising quality of that teaching, reflected in outstanding assessments particularly for education and healthcare, was matched by the calibre of research work being undertaken by students and staff. Maurice Vile was succeeded in 1999 as Director of Research and head of the Graduate School by Professor Alf Smyth, another distinguished academic from UKC, formerly professor of medieval history. He played a key role in preparing Christ Church for the Research Assessment Exercise conducted in 2001, establishing a greater breadth of research. As a result, the RAE rated research in three subject areas as of international and national importance and four more as of national importance. In the previous year Christ Church had gained recognition from the NHS as an official research sponsor.

By the time Christ Church submitted its application for university status, well over 80 per cent of all staff working more than half-time had a doctorate or other higher degree while in excess of 90 per cent of staff in education and healthcare had at least one professional qualification. Many were leading members of their professional associations or carried out other academic-related tasks outside Christ Church. New staff recruited to Christ Church were expected to have qualifications equivalent to those demanded by any university while existing staff often gained promotion to long-established universities. Sean Greenwood soon lost his lonely position as Christ Church's only professor – by 2004 there were 22 professors and 11 readers. All staff

Above left: Ex-international cricket star, Henry Olonga, visited Canterbury Christ Church Gifted and Talented Summer School to give an inspirational talk to some of the UK's most high-achieving school children, 2004

Above right: Working with Save the Children. In recent years, the University has also developed increasingly strong links with south India. The initial contact with the Goodwill Children's Home has now extended to include a hospital and colleges of education catering especially for poor and disadvantaged communities. Working in India has proved a transforming experience for the staff and students involved.

were expected to carry out research and publish the results. Such work, covering topics from citizenship education and marine resource management to the youth justice system and the effectiveness of the health visitor service, also attracted valuable external funding. In relation to graduate research, the number of doctorates on offer steadily increased, as did the number of completed PhDs, rising from 17 in 1999 to more than 100 in 2005. As one member of staff put it, in terms of research Christ Church had moved in two decades from the standards of a higher education college to those merited by a university.

Under the leadership of Margaret Alfrey and, from 2002, Sonia Blandford, who joined Christ Church from the Institute of Education at Oxford Brookes University, the faculty of education (as it became in 1998) sustained an outstanding reputation in its field and continued to account for more than a third of all students. Pioneering work continued, exemplified in the introduction of the Foundation Degree in Child and Youth Studies for classroom assistants in 2000. This was achieved in partnership with the Urban Learning Foundation and the first graduates in 2004 all came from Newham, one of the most disadvantaged of all London boroughs. Many of them then enrolled on the graduate teacher programme in order to win qualified teacher status. The Foundation Degree was also taken up through Christ Church by six other Church colleges, cementing the fruitful relationship between this group of like-minded institutions and making a major contribution in many schools nationwide. A taught doctorate in education was also introduced. The faculty also succeeded in winning national contracts to offer the Gifted and Talented scheme (alongside the universities of Durham, Exeter, Warwick and York) for able school pupils and the Teach First scheme aimed at recruiting promising graduates to teach in inner-city London schools.

Sonia Blandford has extended the faculty's reputation for being in the vanguard of educational thinking and taken it beyond the boundaries of Kent. Today the faculty can claim some involvement in

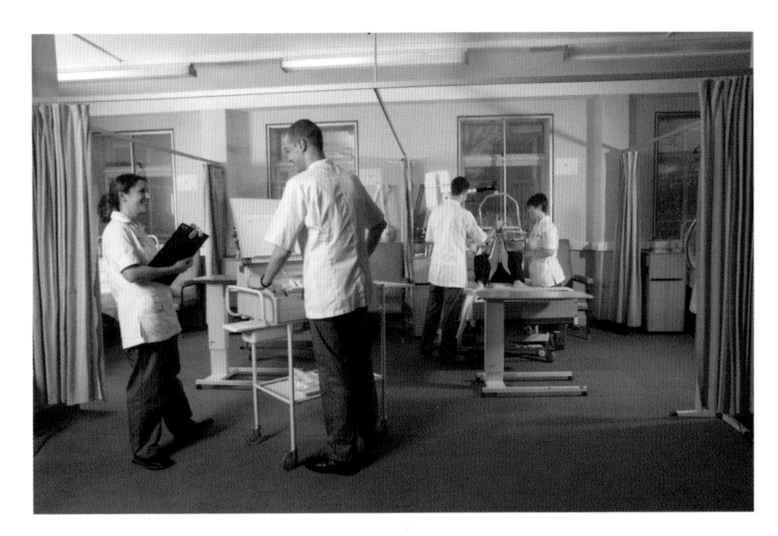

Health and Social Care students in the Skills Laboratory.

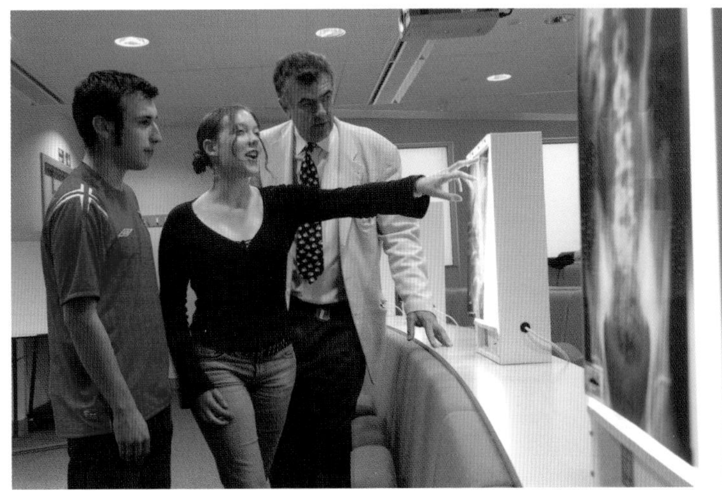

Diagnostic Radiography students gain clinical and academic knowledge through an integrated programme delivered within the department's dedicated practical and laboratory facilities and in Clinical Radiology Departments in Kent and East Sussex.

educational work on every continent except Antarctica. This stretches from Scandinavia and across Europe, reaching throughout Africa and into Asia, China and Australasia, as well as over the Atlantic into the USA, Canada and South America, on projects ranging from teacher training to curriculum regeneration, continuing professional development and extending learning practices. It is an outstanding achievement and one of which Christ Church's founding fathers would have been very proud.

But education is not the only shining star in the Christ Church firmament. The doctorate in clinical psychology, offered as a College degree at Salomons since 1998 under the supervision of Professor Tony Lavender as Director of Accredited Programmes, received an outstanding appraisal from the British Psychological Association. Courses in health and social care continued to receive glowing assessments under Peta Allen and Margaret Andrews, receiving the

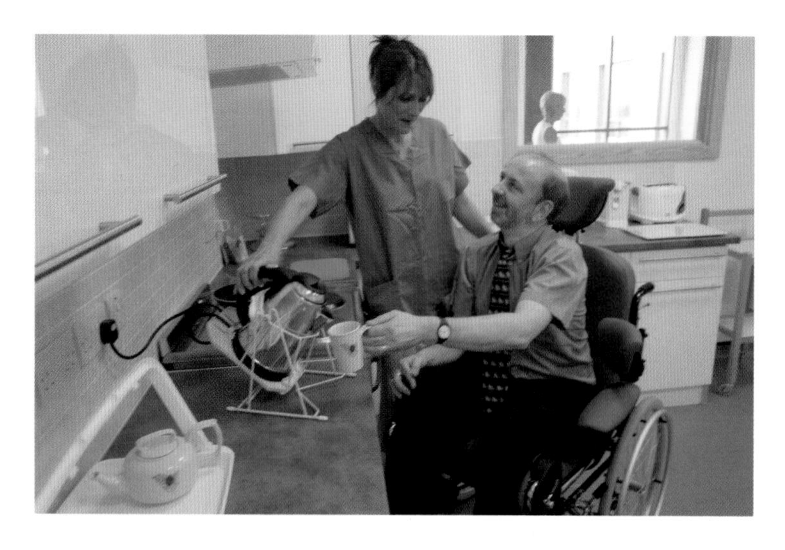

The Occupational Therapy Programme incorporates practice experience undertaken in purpose-built accommodation at the University.

highest possible ranking from the QAA in 2005. The key trend was the move towards closer practical collaboration between the professions. This emerged from a series of critical independent reports into a number of high-profile cases which reflected adversely on the relationship between the professions involved. At Christ Church, the principle that 'you can't work together if you don't learn together' had already been emphasised by the introduction in 1992 under Hazel Colyer of an MSc in Interprofessional Health and Community Studies, an initiative well ahead of its time. In 2000 this was followed by the interprofessional course leading to the Advanced Certificate in Public Health Practice, aimed at community nurses, environmental health officers and others involved in public health. Margaret Andrews, who joined Canterbury in 2001 from the North East Wales Institute, embarked on the creation of an integrated faculty of health and social care and with her colleagues enthusiastically promoted the concept of interprofessional working. This led in September 2004 to the introduction of a pre-registration interprofessional learning programme, involving a new Shared Learning BSc in healthcare.

Other developments included the opening of healthcare skills labs at Canterbury, Broadstairs and Medway as record numbers of students applied for health and social care courses. Funded by the NHS, these courses ranged from occupational therapy, nursing and midwifery to radiography and social work. In addition, HEFCE, in collaboration with employers such as the Kent Association for the Blind, financed foundation degrees with joint teaching programmes. Partnerships such as these have always been one of the strengths of Christ Church. Other examples within the health and social care faculty included collaboration with Brighton University on a degree in community health nursing and the joint teaching of nurses with Greenwich University on the Medway campus. With two degree intakes every year, Christ Church has provided a seamless supply of skilled practitioners to the NHS although the unpredictability of the NHS's workforce planning can pose a challenge. The trend towards greater professionalism in public services, which had begun so long ago with teaching and then, based on that expertise, led Christ Church into a successful relationship with the NHS, was now being embraced by the police. Christ Church, in association with Kent Constabulary, had made a success of the part-time degree in policing introduced in 1997. This was based around the Centre for Studies in Policing which quickly established links with other forces, not only within the UK but also from overseas. The courses devised by Christ Church were soon being studied by police officers in London, Liverpool and Dorset. Alongside the original degree course were added others, for example in forensic investigation and applied criminology, as well as a range of certificates and diplomas, partly aimed at attracting more young people into policing. The full-time foundation degree was launched in 2004 with 220 students, divided across four intakes and between the campuses at Canterbury and Medway. This was a completely new way of conducting initial police training for new recruits and attracted national attention.

Art and music, under David Shutt, the Director of Painting, and Grenville Hancox, Professor of Music, remained vibrant. One exciting initiative, stemming from an opportunity spotted by David Shutt, was the opening in 2004 of the Sidney Cooper Gallery. Named after a

David Shutt, left, and Michael Wright at the opening of the Sidney Cooper Gallery in Canterbury, 2004.

popular and prolific 19th-century Kent artist, the gallery, sited in the heart of the city, hosts a wide variety of exhibitions and shows in a building bought in 2000 by the College and refurbished. As for music, while much-needed improved facilities were being planned, the St Gregory's Centre became the principal music venue, providing a showcase for the College's many talented young musicians. Alongside the Maxwell Davies string quartets which continued to be premiered at the College, a special commission from John Tavener, 'Maha Maya', was performed by the College's Cantata Choir during the 2004 Canterbury Festival as part of the University's 40th birthday celebrations (it had been commissioned in the birthday year of 2002). The limelight was shared by the media department whose Powell Research Centre mounted an exhibition, festival and conference in the same year dedicated to Michael Powell, with the distinguished director and actor, Lord Attenborough, attending the first night. Such displays as these ensured that the strengthening reputation of Christ Church for professional education did not obscure the depth of talent elsewhere. The history department, for instance, one of the outstanding departments in Christ Church for so long, offers a holistic approach, covering medieval, early modern and modern history, one which is fast fading from departments elsewhere but which has proved very popular with students. But innovation sits alongside convention within the liberal arts with equal success, demonstrated by the foundation degrees in the performing arts, commercial music and the digital media. As already noted, English at Christ Church offers not just the usual joint and single honours degree courses but, in association with the Catholic University of Lille, a pioneering double degree. This combination of enthusiasm, talent, quality and innovation across the spectrum ensures that the liberal arts continue to have a valid place within the Christ Church curriculum.

The Sidney Cooper Gallery, Canterbury.

The calibre of Christ Church's science departments is evident from the nature of the research work being done. Projects have covered the application of GIS (Geographic Information Service) to world fisheries, the conservation of birds of prey, water pollution and the role of physical education and sport in schools. Within business and science, where Hall Place has created a focal point for some of the more exciting initiatives, the inclination to break out of the campus boundaries, so characteristic of many aspects of Christ Church today, is obviously apparent. Another project captured the public imagination in 2004 by helping international lorry drivers to overcome language barriers through a series of prompt cards for the most useful phrases. Equally important is the Kent Innovation Centre, run in partnership with Thanet District Council at Broadstairs, where serviced business space is provided for new or growing businesses.

The extending range of Christ Church across several different sites and with ever more students was a huge challenge for the College's library services. It was met, often in the face of considerable hurdles, through Angela Conyers, the director of library services from 1990 until 2003, and her team. They oversaw the introduction of two major library information systems, spearheaded various extensions and expansions and pressed for increased staffing and book stock. A major milestone was the production of the first information strategy, the creation of a website and the provision of electronic information systems across the various campuses. The growth of the library reflected the scale of Christ Church's expansion, from 30,000 books on one site in 1971 to 280,000 spread over four sites in 2005.

There were similar challenges for the College's computing operations under Adrian Wheal and his staff. It was a massive task to wire up all the campuses, building up a network of some 2,500 personal computers, providing general computer training and introducing electronic learning methods. The success with which this was accomplished led the College to be entrusted with developing the regional educational technology network for Kent.

Admissions too met the challenge of expansion where the central admissions unit at the College, under Tony McCulloch and then John Slater and their teams, produced all the necessary publicity, organised visits to schools and fairs and was actively involved in student selection.

The computing facilities.

GOVERNING

It was clear to Michael Wright that the way in which Christ Church had been run in the past had to change. The expansion of the College demanded greater delegation from the centre and effective formal structures which helped to improve inter-departmental co-ordination and cooperation. The result in 1998 was the creation of a series of faculties under the direction of deans with executive responsibilities reporting to a small senior management team headed by the Principal. Over the ensuing years the initial proposals were refined. In 2001 the original seven faculties were reduced to four – Education, Arts and Humanities, Health and Social Care, and Business and Sciences – whose deans were responsible for financial administration and budgeting, plus the associate faculty at Salomons. As well as integrating several departments more closely within the rest of the College, the faculty system also provided greater opportunities for academic staff to become involved in the running of the College.

The Governing Body, 2007. Front row left to right: Canon John Smith, Michael Wright (Vice Chancellor), Bishop Stephen Venner (Pro-Chancellor), Peter Hermitage (Deputy Pro-Chancellor), Dennis Hayes and Paul Bogle (Clerk). Middle row left to right: Tony McDonald, Rupert Bristow, Caroline Spencer, Jean Bannister, Canon Clare Edwards, Susan Price and Peter Abbotts. Back row left to right: David Kemp, Stephen Clark, Roddy Loder-Symonds, Rebecca Heard and Leyland Ridings. (Not present in the photograph: the Reverend Janina Ainsworth, Graham Badman, Colin Carmichael, Barbara Robertson, Paul Sims, Richard Sturt, Dame Janet Trotter.)

Expansion made financial management increasingly important and this was in the capable hands of Bill Taylor until 1995, when Roger Clayton was appointed as Assistant Principal (Business). On Clayton's departure in 2005, his responsibilities were taken over by the newly appointed Strategic Director (Resources), Andrew Ironside (formerly Chief Executive of Salomons).

The governing body was also subject to change, becoming a company limited by guarantee in 2003, when the Church of England finally transferred ownership of land and buildings to Christ Church. A governing body of 25, including six Church nominees, was now a body with strength in depth drawn from business, public service and the professions. Individual governors have become better informed, especially through the greater use of committees to deal with specific areas of governance, including finance. Among distinguished governors who retired during this period were Sir William Taylor, formerly director of the ULIE, as well as a previous Vice Chancellor of the University of Hull and Professor of Education at Bristol, and Brigadier Maurice Atherton, who led the governing body until 1999. His successor was Dr John Bragg, whose career had been spent in the pharmaceutical industry and, after retirement, as the chairman of several local health authorities. He was tireless in his encouragement of the College's pursuit of university status which was achieved before he stepped down in the summer of 2005. He was succeeded by the Bishop of Dover, Stephen Venner, also the Vice-Chairman of the Church of England Board of Education, who became the new University's first Pro-Chancellor. Among the longest serving of the University's governors was Professor John Todd of the University of Kent, who stepped down in 2007 after 15 years.

Senior Management Team and Officers. Front row left to right: Jan Druker, Margaret Andrews, Michael Wright, Sue Piotrowski and Sonia Blandford. Back row left to right: David Leah, Paul Dalton, Tony Lavender, Keith Gwilym, Andrew Ironside and Paul Bogle.

Living

The College as it grew retained its Anglican ethos through the hard work and commitment of successive chaplains, and latterly in particular through Jeremy Law as Dean of Chapel. Administering to so many students spread over so wide an area was a challenge, met in part through welcome services for students, support for student Christian groups and international students, weekly services and prayer meetings, pastoral work, the promotion of charitable service and initiatives such as text-a-prayer. All this, combined with the continuing central focus of the chapel and the looming presence of the cathedral, contributed towards the warm, tolerant and collegiate atmosphere of the Canterbury campus which the College sought to export to Christ Church's newer outposts.

As Jeremy Law wrote in 2004,

> *a huge part of the Christian tradition is about hospitality and unconditional welcome. It is also about the search for what is true and, therefore, we encourage everybody to engage in that search without necessarily enforcing what answers they are going to find.*

Testimony to this spirit came in the student magazine in 2003 from a female student from Chicago, who was full of praise for the welcome she had received from students and staff at Christ Church during her three-month stay.

The Union was another bastion of student support which worked closely with the College, especially in partnership with the Dean of

Open air service at St Augustine's Abbey, 2004.

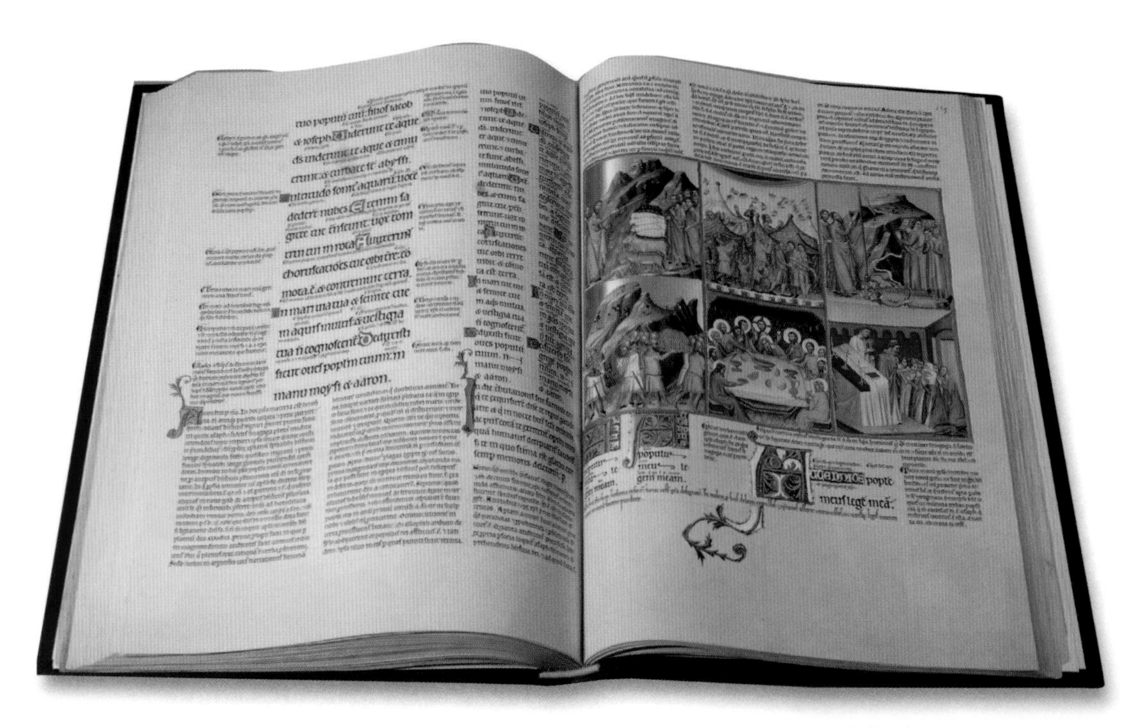

Students, a post filled in 1998 by Sue Piotrowski. Both had to face the same challenge, of meeting the needs of an ever larger and more diverse body of students. As one annual report remarked, 'students at Christ Church demonstrate the reality of lifelong learning'. Mature students studied alongside students coming straight from school. More than half of all students were part-time. Only a thousand of Christ Church's 14,000 students were resident. Many lived close to their chosen campus and drove in every morning. Older students often had families or other responsibilities beyond the campus. Students themselves began to assume increasing responsibility for the financial cost of higher education, with most of them taking part-time jobs during term to pay their way. Degrees also became more and more the usual requirement for professional careers. All this made students inclined to take a more demanding view of the quality of the education they were being offered. Student life was perhaps less frivolous, with less time for passionate involvement in the political issues of the day and participation in student organisations.

Christ Church has lived up to student expectations. The partnership between the University and its students won plaudits in the 2005 Institutional Audit Report by the Quality Assurance Agency. A Student Forum, chaired by Sue Piotrowski, was established as a body where student representatives and senior staff could exchange views. This was backed up by departmental staff–student liaison committees and by the widespread use of electronic communication to consult with students and keep them informed. This has been particularly important

Canterbury Christ Church acquired a copy of the magnificent Book of Psalms, the Great Canterbury Psalter in 2005. The original Psalter was created at Canterbury Cathdral in the 12th century.

A group of alumni who were among the first students at the College donated a bench with a brass plaque in 2005 to commemorate the founding staff and students. Hilary Hardcastle, the first Vice-President of the Students' Union said, 'Our cohort was a very special group… the majority of us went on to become teachers, head teachers and key figures in education. We have so many memories of teaching and learning together. Those days at Christ Church College were idyllic ones and they will be treasured by us always.'

for an institution which is spread over several campuses and has helped to sustain the strong collegiate ethos throughout the University. But as well as formal mechanisms, students are always encouraged to contact the chair of the Student Forum directly with any issues of general concern. In addition, special efforts have been made to build the confidence of students during that difficult first year of university to ensure that as many as possible stay on to complete their courses. Christ Church has conducted triennial student surveys and the last of these, in 2004, had a response rate of 86 per cent from the selected sample of students and showed that three-quarters were very satisfied with the quality of the teaching at Christ Church. The University was also involved in establishing the National Student Survey. In 2006 this survey, which takes into account the views of final-year students in areas such as teaching, academic support, learning resources and personal development, placed Christ Church among the top universities and colleges in the country, alongside institutions such as LSE, Imperial College and the University of Manchester.

All this, combined with the quality of the education offered by Christ Church, produced a drop-out rate lower than the national average, the consistent achievement of first-class and upper-second-class degrees by half of all students and a graduate unemployment rate of just three per cent. Christ Church has been among the top 20 higher education institutions for success in placing graduates in employment or further study within six months of graduation. While the entry requirements for many subjects at Christ Church are not high – although some subjects are in great demand, allowing only the most able to gain places – it is one of Christ Church's distinctive features that it has achieved such success with so many of its students. As a University, Christ Church is increasingly popular, drawing more students not only from more distant parts of the UK but also from overseas.

Students have benefited from the investment made by the University in recent years, such as the improved refectory, better library and IT services. The Union's lament has been that much still needs to be done, in providing a Union building able to cater for such a large and diverse constituency, in improving existing facilities, such as the limited sporting provision, and in establishing an effective student support network and facilities across all locations. These aspirations are also shared by the University.

Students also have the benefit of the advice of specialist financial and disability advisers. Christ Church secured special funding in 1999 for improved disabled provision which also covered various physical improvements. Through numerous campaigns by the Union, students have also been made aware of issues such as sexual health, eating disorders, meningitis, mental health, dyslexia, drugs and smoking, finance, and student discipline. Dealing with these issues was also helped by the funding of a sabbatical Union officer for welfare and education. Other concerns ranged from accommodation – or the lack of it – to neighbourliness. One initiative intended to foster the latter was 'Silent Students, Happy Homes', introduced by the Union in partnership with the city council.

Below: Current students v 'old boys' rugby and football, 2007.

A sports and societies officer was another new sabbatical appointment. By 2002, for instance, there were 35 sports clubs and ten societies active within Christ Church. Although participation was sometimes restricted because so many students were mature and part-time, with another life beyond the campus, these clubs and societies catered for a wide range of interests. Among the stronger sports were men's basketball, men's and women's football and hockey, women's rugby, cricket, netball, lacrosse, squash and volleyball. Some sports, such as men's football, ran several

Above left: Canterbury Student Radio.

Below left: Current students v 'old girls' rugby, 2007.

Above right and next page: The Summer Ball's attractions included a full size fairground, complete with dodgems and a ghost train. The Christ Church Students' Union Summer Ball is the event that rounds off the year, and in June 2007 over 1,500 students partied the night away.

teams. There were also a number of outstanding individual successes, notably James Williams' membership of the 1998 Commonwealth Games gold-medal-winning fencing team. The strongest societies included the student radio station (C4), the music societies, such as the chamber choir and orchestra, and drama. C4 finally came to an end in 2006 but was replaced by CSR (Canterbury Student Radio), a joint venture with UKC, the only student-led radio station to be granted an FM community radio licence in the UK. Two highlights in every academic year remain Rag Week, when thousands of pounds are raised for charity, and the Summer Ball, which has established a consistent reputation as having the best line-up of live bands in the country.

Life for students and academic staff in today's University would be impossible to sustain without the help from that unsung army of ancillary staff, whether it is the catering staff who provide hundreds of meals every day of every term, or the grounds staff who make the Canterbury campus a pleasure all year round, or the invaluable support of the head porter, Alan Connolly, and his team. Another example is Jan Bowman, for many years the personal assistant to Michael Berry and then Michael Wright, whose self-effacing modesty belied her key contribution to the smooth running of Christ Church. Too often taken for granted, the vital contribution of people like these would soon be missed if it was taken away. And today they are recognised perhaps more than they have ever been as an integral part of the University's staff.

Conclusion

Although the first students entered Christ Church only in 1962, the University as a Church foundation can lay claim to traditions stretching back centuries. The Anglican ethos remains at the heart of the University today and can be seen in much of what Christ Church has already achieved and seeks to achieve in the future. There is the way in which the University embraces students of so many different backgrounds, nationalities and beliefs, and strives with such consistent success to unlock often hidden potential. There is the belief of staff, as one remarked, 'in the power of education to change the lives of the students who come here'; 'there is great excitement in seeing people grow in such a short period of time … [in seeing such] an explosion of development'. Visitors can feel this vigour and excitement in every part of the University, whether at Canterbury, Salomons, Broadstairs or Medway.

Yet at the same time there is also a tangible warmth and friendliness, and a tolerant, supportive and welcoming atmosphere. Although there are now more than 14,000 students in the University, Christ Church has successfully resisted the anonymity of many large organisations. These characteristics are not things which have magically appeared overnight. They have been shared by every successive generation of students and staff since the foundation of the University. To repeat the words used by the Archdeacon of Maidstone as chairman of the governing body in 1962, Christ Church is a place where students 'may find in their own fellowship in the College, and in chapel and in relations with the staff, a rich expression of Christian community living'.

Staff and students in the garden at St Martin's Priory, Canterbury.

Left: The Canterbury Cross in the courtyard of the Broadstairs campus.

The foundation of the University stemmed from the historic involvement of the Church in education. The University remains at the forefront of delivering the training of teachers as a vital contribution to the social life of the nation. Moreover, Christ Church has brought this expertise in professional training to bear on other equally vital aspects of national life, in healthcare, social work and policing. This active involvement in the life of the nation created an outward-looking organisation. Students are sent out to teach in the schools of Kent, to work in the county's hospitals or to police the county, as part of their studies. Today the University also shares this invaluable accumulated experience with other institutions and organisations not only throughout the UK but increasingly overseas. At the same time Christ Church, through its involvement with the wider community, has also taken the opportunity to extend the benefits of higher education at Broadstairs, Tunbridge Wells, Medway and Folkestone, as well as through the links it has with the Urban Learning Foundation. The University has also played a positive part in the life of the local community, through its contribution in music and the arts, through student teams taking part in local leagues and through its links with Canterbury Cathedral. Much of this has been achieved in partnership with others, whether local education authorities or the NHS, colleges and universities at home or overseas, businesses or community groups. Distinguished members of the wider community have influenced the work of the University through membership of the governing body.

The possibility that Christ Church might achieve university status must have seemed extraordinarily remote during the difficult days of the 1970s. Then it seemed that the College might become just another name on a long casualty list. Flexibility, adaptability, entrepreneurial drive, combined with vision, commitment and determination, enabled Christ Church firstly to survive and then to expand. All those qualities, rare then, widely emulated now, remain in evidence today and have become part of the University's character. They will go a long way towards the University meeting future challenges. One will be to reconcile the competing pressures arising from the University's increasing popularity, rising student expectations, the need to sustain excellence in key areas and raise standards in others as well as to maintain a commitment to provide as wide an access to higher education as possible. All this has an inevitable impact on long-term planning, the use of space and the management of the University's existing campus network. At home, the University must consolidate its position as a leading regional participant in regeneration through higher education, while there is still much to do in furthering the University's international links. There may also be opportunities to apply the University's skills in professional training to additional public services. In the face of all this, perhaps the key challenge of the future will be for Christ Church to maintain the distinctive identity which has been such an important part of its success.

The University has grown rapidly during the past four and a half decades yet still manages to retain a friendly, welcoming environment for students, staff and visitors alike.

Appendices

Chancellors

Dr Rowan Williams The Most Reverend and Right Honourable the Lord Archbishop of Canterbury	2005–

Chairmen of the Govering Body

The Venerable R Gordon Strutt Archdeacon of Maidstone	1961–1965
Dr Geoffrey Templeman	1966–1987
Dr Richard Third The Right Reverend the Bishop of Dover	1988–1992
Dr William Petty	1992–1994
Brigadier Maurice A Atherton	1994–1999
Dr H John Bragg	1999–2005
Stephen Venner (Pro-Chancellor) The Right Reverend the Bishop of Dover	2005–

Principals

The Reverend Dr Frederic Mason	1962–1975
Dr Michael Berry	1975–1997
Professor Michael Wright (Vice Chancellor from 2005)	1997–

Vice Principals

Vivien Young	1962–1973
Dr Michael Berry	1973–1975
Ruth-Mary Walker	1975–1985
Dr Graham Brown	1985–1995
Professor Alan Hay	1995–2002
Professor Chris Bounds (Deputy Vice Chancellor from 2005)	2002–2005

Honorary Fellows

Brigadier Maurice Atherton CBE
Professor Chris Bounds
Dr H John Bragg
Dr Graham Brown
The Right Reverend and Right Honourable Lord Carey of Clifton
Mr Chandu Christian
Mr Nicolas Cleobury
Mr David Coupe
Mr Roger De Haan
Mrs Sylvia Denton OBE
The Right Honourable Baroness Emerton DBE DL
The Right Honourable Frank Field MP
Sir John Grugeon
Dame Kelly Holmes
The Right Honourable Lord Kingsdown
The Right Reverend John Richard Llewellin
Sir Peter Maxwell-Davies
Mrs Geraldine McCaughrean
The Maggini Quartet
Mr Ken Moran
The Reverend Dame Sarah Mullally DBE
Sir David Phillips QPM
Professor Richard Pring
Lady Joan Reid
Mr Gary Rhodes OBE
Councillor Jenny Samper
The Most Reverend and Right Honourable Dr John Sentamu
The Very Reverend John Simpson
Mr Peter Smallridge CBE
Professor Sir William Taylor OBE
Dame Janet Trotter
Mr Noel Vallely
The Most Reverend Gregory Venables
Professor Maurice Vile
Mr Allan Willett CMG
Mr Peter Williams
The Very Reverend Robert Willis

INDEX

Italics indicates pictures

Abbotts, Peter *126*
Alfrey, Margaret 52, *77*, 120
Allen, Peta 76, *77*, 121
Andrews, Margaret 121, 122, *127*
Armstrong-Jones, H 39, 40
Atherton, Brigadier Maurice 96, 127, 140, 141
Attenborough, Lord 124
Ayckbourn, Alan 66

Bannister, Jean *126*
Becket, St Thomas 96
Berry, Dr Michael 28, 29, 30, 45, 48, 50, 51, 52, 53, 54, 55, 56, 59, 68, 71, *71*, 74, 81, 87, 94, 96, 110, 133, 140
Blandford, Sonia 120, *127*
Blanthorn, Jim 30, 71
Bogle, Paul *126*, *127*
Bounds, Chris 103, 110, 140, 141
Bowman, Jan 133
Bragg, Dr John 127, 140, 141
Brazier, Julian 88
Bristow, Rupert *126*
Brown, Dr Graham 48, 51, 52, 54, 68, 70, 71, 74, 76, 87, 94, 140, 141

Carey, Dr George (Lord Carey of Clifton) 90, 141
Christian, Chandu 141
Clark, Stephen *126*
Clayton, Roger 104, 127
Cleobury, Nicholas 141
Clifford-Amos, Dr Terence *79*, 82, 88
Clift, Dr Stephen 53, 106
Cockin, Bishop 16, 21
Colyer, Hazel 122
Connolly, Alan *111*, 133
Conyers, Angela 125
Coupe, David 58, 82, 85, 114, 141

David, Tricia 96
Dalton, Paul *127*
Dayes, Edward 14
De Haan, Roger 106, 141
Denton, Sylvia 141
Diaper, Gordon 81
Druker, Jan *126*

Edwards, Canon Clare *126*
Edwards, Tony 40, 96
Emerton, Baroness 141

Field, Frank 141
Flight, A L (Alf) 39
Fricker, Dr Frank *30*

Gibson, James 39
Goodenough, Richard 80
Greenwood, Sean 42, 80, 118
Grugeon, Sir John 141
Gwilym, Keith 71, *96*, *127*

Hancox, Grenville *48*, 66, 90, 106, 123
Hardcastle, Hilary 131
Harvey, Nikki 96
Hay, Alan 140
Hayes, Dennis *126*
Heard, Rebecca *126*
Hermitage, Peter *111*, *126*
Herring 37
Hetherington, Tom 30, 42
Holmes, Dame Kelly 141
Holt, David 25, *25*

Ironside, Andrew 127, *127*

Jenkins, Peter 34, 38, *38*
Joseph, Sir Keith 55
Jukes, Francis 14

Kemp, David *126*
Kendall, Lorna 36, 39
Kent Constabulary *97*
Kingsdown, Lord 141
Kirkham, W J 39
Knight, A R (Reg) 30, *30*

Lavender, Professor Tony 121, *127*
Law, Jeremy 128
Leah, David *127*
Lewis, Shalley 36
Llewellin, John Richard 141
Loder-Symonds, Roddy *126*

Marshall, Johnson 22
Mason, Dr Frederic *17*, 18, *18*, 21, 28, 30, 31, 32, 35, 37, 38, 39, 40, 41, 42, 43, 45, 140
Matthew, Robert 22
Maxwell Davies, Sir Peter *90*, 141

McCaughrean, Geraldine 141
McCulloch, Peter *31*
McCulloch, Tony 125
McCulloch, Mrs *31*
McDonald, Tony *126*
Milne, Nikki 91
Moran, Ken 141
Moss, Dr John *79*
Mullally, Dame Sarah 141

Olonga, Henry *120*

Petty, Dr William 96, 140
Phillips, Sir David 141
Piotrowski, Sue 106, *127*, 130
Powell, Michael 112, 114, *114*, 124
Pressburger, Emeric 114, *114*
Price, Susan *126*
Priestly, J B 66
Pring, Richard 141

Ramsey, Dr Michael *17*, 32, 39
Reid, Lady Joan 141
Rhodes, Gary 141
Richards, Dan *114*
Ridings, Leyland *126*
Rusholme, Lord James of 42
Russell, Miss 37

Salomons, Sir David Lionel 86, *86*
Salomons, Sir David 84, 86, *86*, 115
Samper, Jenny 141
Scott, Sir Giles Gilbert 56
Sentamu, Dr John 141
Shakespeare, William 66
Shutt, David 123, *123*
Simpson, John 141
Slater, John 125
Smallridge, Peter 141
Smith, Canon John *126*
Smyth, Alf 118
Spencer, Caroline *126*
St Charles, Aragon 96
Stears, David 53
Strutt, Gordon 21, 140

Tavener, John 124
Taylor, Bill 71, 127
Taylor, Sir William 127, 141
Tee, Lynsey 96
Templeman, Dr Geoffrey 30, 31, 37, 43, 45, 68, 140
Third, Dr Richard 140
Thomas, Allyn *97*
Todd, Professor John 127
Trotter, Dame Janet 141
Turmeau, William 100
Tyler, Miss 37

Vallely, Noel 141
Venables, Gregory 141
Venner, Stephen *111*, *126*, 127, 140
Vile, Maurice 50, 55, 81, 118, 141

Wagg, Michael 34
Wake, Clive 88
Walker, Ruth-Mary 140
Watson, Norman 40
Wellard, Mrs *18*
Wheal, Adrian 125
Whitaker, Mabel 36, 39, *39*
Wilde, Oscar 66
Wilder, Thornton 66
Willett, Allan 141
Williams, Dr Rowan *111*, 140
Williams, James 133
Williams, Peter 141
Willis, Robert 141
Wiseman, Simon 91
Wootton, Lady 84
Wright, Michael 6, 100, *100*, 102, 103, 104, *108*, 110, *111*, 116, *123*, 126, *126*, *127*, 133

Young, Vivien *17*, 30, *31*, 36, 140

Photo Acknowledgements

Every effort has been made to contact the copyright holders of all works reproduced in this book. However, if acknowledgements have been omitted, the publishers ask those concerned to contact James & James (Publishers) Ltd, a member of the TMI Group.

Canterbury Christ Church University would like to extend special thanks to David King Photographer for the provision of various archived images and the majority of new photography commissioned for this publication. Also thanks to Kent Messenger Group, Lee Robinson, John Pollock, Robert Berry, Paul Knivett, Andrew Goodenough, Studio 2 design & photography studios.

Corbis: Saker Falcon Perched Upon a Rock © Eric and David Hosking, p 81.
BFI: Powell and Pressburger, p 114; The Life and Death of Colonel Blimp poster, p114; The Red Shoes, p 114.